THE RAIN AND SNOW COME DOWN FROM THE HEAVENS AND STAY ON THE GROUND TO WATER THE EARTH. THEY CAUSE THE GRAIN TO GROW, PRODUCING SEED FOR THE FARMER AND BREAD FOR THE HUNGRY. IT IS THE SAME WITH MY WORD. I SEND IT OUT, AND IT ALWAYS PRODUCES FRUIT. IT WILL ACCOMPLISH ALL I WANT IT TO, AND IT WILL PROSPER EVERYWHERE I SEND IT.

ISAIAH 55:10-11

EXECUTIVE SUMMARY OF THE BIBLE

CHAPLAIN FARRIS AND RUTH ROBERTSON

Executive Summary of the Bible
By Chaplain Farris and Ruth Robertson

Published by
Recovery Literature
217 West Bennett Street
Springfield, Missouri 65807
(417) 208-5990
www.RecoveryLiterature.com

ISBN-13: 978-0911939019
ISBN-10: 0911939016
Library of Congress Control Number: 2013903153

Printed in the United States of America.

TABLE OF CONTENTS

All timeline dates are approximate.

TABLE OF FIGURES

An asterisk (*) denotes public domain Bible Illustrations by French Artist Gustave Doré, 1832-1883.

Double Asterisks (**) denote public domain maps of both Old and New Testament Bible times from the *Atlas of the Historical Geography of the Holy Land* by George Adam Smith and J. G. Bartholomew, London, 1915.

INTRODUCTION

The Bible is the most bought and least understood book on earth. For the number of Bibles sold each year, one might think there would be a great deal of Bible knowledge among us, but that is not the case. We could cite numerous studies that all prove the same thing: Mankind is still only vaguely aware of what is contained in the greatest selling book the earth has ever known.

There are many reasons for this indisputable fact. Generally speaking, we have obstacles that keep us from reading the Bible, but we also have obstacles that keep us from understanding the Bible. We are convinced that if it were easier to understand the Bible, then people would be more willing to read it. Therefore, our simple goal is to make it easier for you to read and understand the Bible.

We have no desire to have you subscribe to our interpretation of the Bible. We believe the Spirit of God will instruct you in these matters as you honestly seek the truth. We only want to make it easier for you to see what God says in the Bible. We will therefore limit our discussion to the widely accepted canon of scripture recognized by Christians throughout the world. Once armed with this knowledge, you may then engage in discussions about spiritual matters on a wide array of Bible basics. You will also become equipped to review your life and compare yourself to the spiritual giants and villains of the Bible. Overall, you will become competent in spiritual affairs.

You will need to be patient with yourself in this process. There are times when your very own mind will want to veer left or right from the information being presented. We urge you to quiet your mind and search your soul for the desire to experience God. You will get inspired at times to investigate a particular issue in more depth. Don't be discouraged! Keep a Bible nearby and don't be afraid to take a break and search the internet and explore the questions that arise in your mind.

You may feel overwhelmed by the vastness of the subjects at hand. You may find yourself wanting instead to focus on your less complicated daily activities. You may want to put off spiritual matters that are challenging and frustrating. Again, be patient, take a short break as needed, but stay true to the adventure. Your learning about the ways of God is meant to last your entire lifetime. It is not a phase or a fad to suit your whimsy. We urge you to become a student of God for life.

Many brilliant scientists, sociologists, business and world leaders believe in God and believe the Bible is the inerrant word of God. Keep an open mind, study this Executive Summary of the Bible, read the Bible of your choosing, and engage in further studies in areas that peak your interest. The more you learn, the easier it becomes to believe in God the Creator, even though you may have lifelong questions that remain unanswered.

This book is meant to help you avoid the feeling that you are trudging through quicksand as you try to read and learn. To that end, we urge you set aside your prejudices and preconceived notions. Try to appreciate the overview presented here without getting caught up in the complexities. A childlike faith instead of a critical mind will give you an opportunity to start to understand God's seemingly impossible ways.

Various factions scream loudly, proclaiming their interpretation of life, science, and scripture as the only valid perspective, closing their mind to any alternatives. Forget theology for now. You may currently have beliefs or thoughts that seem to make it impossible to subscribe to a biblical system of belief, but we have often seen those who first scoff remain to pray.

We urge you here and now to resign, at least temporarily, from the great debate society and start with a fresh perspective. Forget everything you have heard about Bible translations and interpretations, get a copy of the Bible that you can read and understand, and keep it alongside you as you read this simple book.

If you happen to already be a believer, there might be additional reasons to read this text: Perhaps you want to gain God's perspective by understanding the scope of His plan for earth; perhaps you don't understand some of the complex pieces of the biblical puzzle and get stuck in the begats and wherefores; perhaps the different nations and tribes and historical settings for events are not yet clear in your mind.

If you are already a Believer, our goal is to give you a bird's eye view of God's plan, demystify the Bible and provide a timeline that will help you understand and enjoy the Bible more fully. Once you have achieved a greater level of confidence in your knowledge about God and life, we trust that you will become a more able co-worker in Christ.

In Exodus 34:10, God selects the Israelites to publicize God's word through "miracles that have never been performed anywhere in all the earth or in any nation." The Israelites were faithful in securing the text of God's word about these miracles for future generations. Jesus has been faithful in manifesting God's word and brought it fully to all mankind. Likewise, the Holy Spirit has been faithful in spreading God's word throughout the world. Now, it is upon each soul, as time quickens, to be the light of truth in a world that is increasingly sophisticated, yet still darkened by ignorance and selfishness.

Think about what I am saying. The Lord will help you understand all these things.

[2 Timothy 2:7]

CHARACTERS OF THE BIBLE

Author and Main Characters

❑ Author: The Bible is a compilation of books. God spoke through at least 40 people, who penned the 66 books of the Bible over a 1500-year time-span. The 66 books of the Bible are divided into two main sections: the Old Testament and the New Testament.

❑ Two primary characters: God and mankind, which includes all humans.

❑ Additional spiritual beings exist as angels, demons, or unknown entities.

❑ Character interactions: The Old Testament focuses on God's building of a people group of faith, the Israelites, as a microcosm for all people groups. The New Testament focuses on God's inclusion of all people by faith, both Israelites and Gentiles (i.e. non-Jews).

❑ God has three manifestations, called the Trinity or Triune God.
   (1) God's Authority is identified as "LORD" or "Father."
   (2) God's Compassion is identified as "The Angel of the Lord," "The Messiah," or "Jesus the Son."
   (3) God's Assistance to mankind is identified as "The Spirit of the Lord" or "The Holy Spirit."

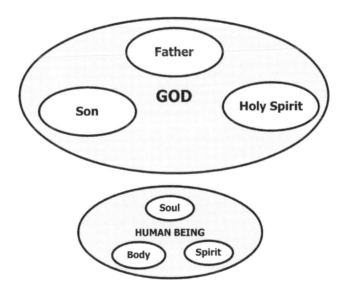

Figure 1: The Triune God and Three aspects of People

❑ Each person has three aspects to their human existence.
   (1) Each person's physical attributes are identified as "strength" or "body."
   (2) Each person's personality, decision-making processes and individuality are identified as "mind" or "soul."
   (3) The communication of each person with a Higher Authority is identified as "heart" or "spirit."

- ❑ There are different categories of significant people on the scene. Sometimes God uses one person to fill more than one role:
    - ○ Patriarchs are the early founders of monotheism who are chosen by God to implement His plan upon the earth. They range from Adam to King David and include Noah, Abraham, Isaac, Moses and the leaders of each tribe of Israel, among others.
    - ○ Prophets are those people inspired directly by God to speak the truth to His people. They range from Moses to John the Beloved. There are "major prophets" who have extensive writings that have a major impact on the developing story of God's plan for His people and "minor prophets" who have an equally important message that is shorter and more focused. Prophets are often unpopular because of the message of accountability they bring.
    - ○ Judges are those people who represent God in His safekeeping and administrative concerns for the well being of His people. They often acted as military leaders and are called for a time, usually returning to their family business when not needed to lead during a crisis.
    - ○ Kings are those people who are appointed for life by God or man to lead people. The position of King passes from father to son. There are godly and ungodly Kings. Kings are not limited to biblical people groups.
    - ○ Priests work among people and represent their people group to God. They have religious and sacramental duties that may include hearing confessions or presenting sacrifices to God. There are different orders of priests that have a different emphasis or focus.
    - ○ Disciples are followers of a teacher whom may be called Master.
    - ○ Apostles are people who carry the Master's message out to the world. They are an emissary or ambassador to the Master.
- ❑ There are spiritual beings that are not God or man. Demons are fallen angels, but angels all the same. Angels are referred to as messengers at times. There are also Seraphim, Cherubim, and Four Living Creatures that are more powerful spiritual beings and are thought by many to be angels of a higher order.

Your word is a lamp to guide my feet, and a light for my path.

–Psalm 119:105

PLOT OF THE BIBLE

The Bible is a true story, but it is not a complete history of God, the universe or mankind. All characters and plot, including miracles and unusual circumstances, happened. This chapter provides the chronicle as narrated in the Bible as well as the approximate timeline associated with the action. The Old Testament begins with God's Creation. We date man's creation based upon the general approximate date of 4000 BC which is within close range of the estimation of many biblical scholars.

Timeline	God's Creation
unknown	❑ Day 1: God creates the Heavens and the Earth. The word for heavens means both visible heavenly bodies, as in planets and galaxies, as well as unseen, as in angels in Heaven. Later in the Bible, more information is provided concerning one particular angel, called Satan, who tries to usurp God's authority. God expels Satan and Satan's followers from Heaven, and Satan and his followers take up residence on Earth.
	❑ Day 2: God separates the waters above, Sky, from the waters below, the Earth's Surface. The author's perspective is from the Earth's surface since the sky is above him.
	❑ Day 3: God collects the water to form Sea, separating out the Land, and plants vegetation.
	❑ Day 4: God creates the Sun, the Moon, and the Stars, although from the perspective of the Earth's surface, this means the atmosphere clears, revealing the Sun, the Moon, and the Stars.
	❑ Day 5: God creates Animals in the air, Birds, and Animals in the sea, Fish.
4000 B.C.	❑ Day 6: God creates Animals on Land and the first People, Adam and Eve. God puts Adam in the Garden of Eden, a lush part of the Earth's surface, and God walks with Adam in a physical way.
	❑ Day 7: God Rests.

Figure 2: God creates light.

Timeline	Noah's Ark and the Tower of Babel
	❑ Satan, the angelic enemy of mankind, convinces Adam and Eve to disobey God. As a consequence God expels Adam and Eve from the Garden of Eden. Adam and Eve take up residence in untamed wilderness.
	❑ Adam and Eve have lots of descendants.
	❑ Since people are no longer walking directly with God, as Adam did in the Garden of Eden, it doesn't take long for people to forget about God and start to worship other gods, such as sun, fire, water, or handmade idols.
	❑ God sees wickedness everywhere and singles out Noah as righteous .
2456 B.C.	❑ God floods the Earth, saving only Noah, his family, and a few of each kind of animal in a boat. After about a year in the boat, the ground is dry and the people and animals return to land.
	❑ Since Noah is faithful, God promises never to flood the Earth again. This promise is called the Noahic Covenant and is represented by the rainbow.
2350 B.C.	❑ Once Noah and his descendants are established on dry ground, God commands people to venture out and populate the land. ❑ Instead, people settle in Babylon and build the tower of Babel in an attempt to reach Heaven. ❑ God confuses language so that people scatter to colonize new lands.

Figure 3: God confuses language so that people will spread out and populate the Earth.

Timeline	God's Covenant with Abraham
	❑ People again forget about God and worship other gods.
2166 B.C.	❑ God singles out Abram (renamed Abraham by God) as faithful and righteous.
	❑ God promises that Abraham will father a Nation. This Nation will inhabit the Land of Canaan. This Nation will worship only God. This three-part promise consists of (1) the nation of people; (2) the promised land; and (3) the support of God. This is called the Abrahamic covenant.
2066 B.C.	❑ Abraham has two sons, Isaac and Ishmael. Both are blessed in worldly ways but God's spiritual promise is inherited by Isaac and passed on to Jacob (later renamed Israel), then Israel's future generations. Ishmael is known through extra-biblical sources to be the father of the many Islamic peoples.
2005 B.C.	❑ Isaac has two sons, Jacob (later renamed Israel) and Esau, but God's promise is passed to Jacob/Israel.
	❑ Jacob/Israel has twelve sons, Reuben, Simeon, Levi, Judah, Dan, Naphtali, Gad, Asher, Issachar, Zebulun, Joseph, and Benjamin.
1914 B.C.	❑ Jacob is now renamed Israel, meaning "Struggle with God."
	❑ Each of Jacob's twelve sons heads a family, called a tribe.
1876 B.C.	❑ Per God's plan to build a nation to worship only God, Israel and his twelve sons and their families, all twelve tribes, a total of seventy-five people, move to Egypt. These tribes are now called the Israelites, or Nation of Israel.

Figure 4: Abraham journeys into the land of Canaan.

Timeline	Israelites return to Canaan
	❏ Egyptians, afraid of the quickly-multiplying Israelites, enslave the Israelites.
	❏ After 400 years, there are one million Israelites, still identified by twelve tribes.
	❏ Per the Abrahamic Covenant, the population has been increased, but the land promised to them is Canaan, not Egypt where they are slaves.
1526 B.C.	❏ God sends Moses to lead the Israelites back to Canaan, the promised land.
	❏ On the way, God re-introduces Himself to the Israelites at Mount Sinai.
	❏ Israelites agree to keep God's laws and worship only God, per the Abrahamic Covenant.
1446 B.C.	❏ God provides the Israelites with the Ten Commandments or Laws.

❏ Out of fear, the Israelites do not want God to speak directly to them, and ask Moses to act as intermediary for God's commands.

❏ However, the Israelites do not listen to Moses, and disobey God, and the consequences are that they must spend 40 years in the desert.

❏ Moses predicts that a Greater Prophet will come, to whom the Israelites will listen.

❏ God sets up a system of worship using sacrifices in a portable temple, called the Tabernacle, administered by Aaron, the first High Priest.

❏ Moses writes down God's Law using Hebrew, the language of the Israelites.

❏ Moses dies in the desert, leaving Joshua in charge of the Israelites.

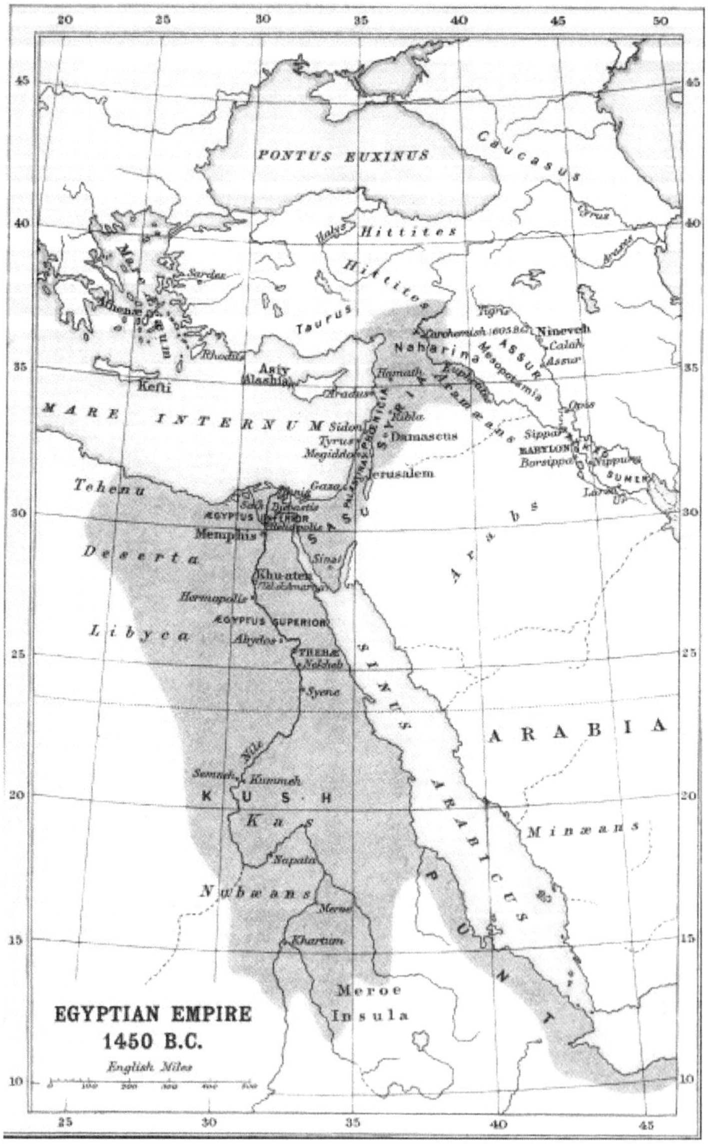

Figure 5: Israelites are slaves in ancient Egypt.

Timeline	Establishment of Israel and Judges
1407 B.C.	❑ Joshua leads Israelites to conquer Canaan and the land is now named Israel. ❑ God leaves some pagans in the land to teach the younger Israelites how to fight. ❑ The pagans will also present a temptation for the Israelites to worship other gods.
1350 B.C.	❑ God appoints a series of judges as leadership for the twelve tribes of Israel. ❑ The spirit of God comes upon each appointed judge, and the judges act as intermediaries for God. ❑ However, during the times between judges, the Israelites sin and worship other gods.

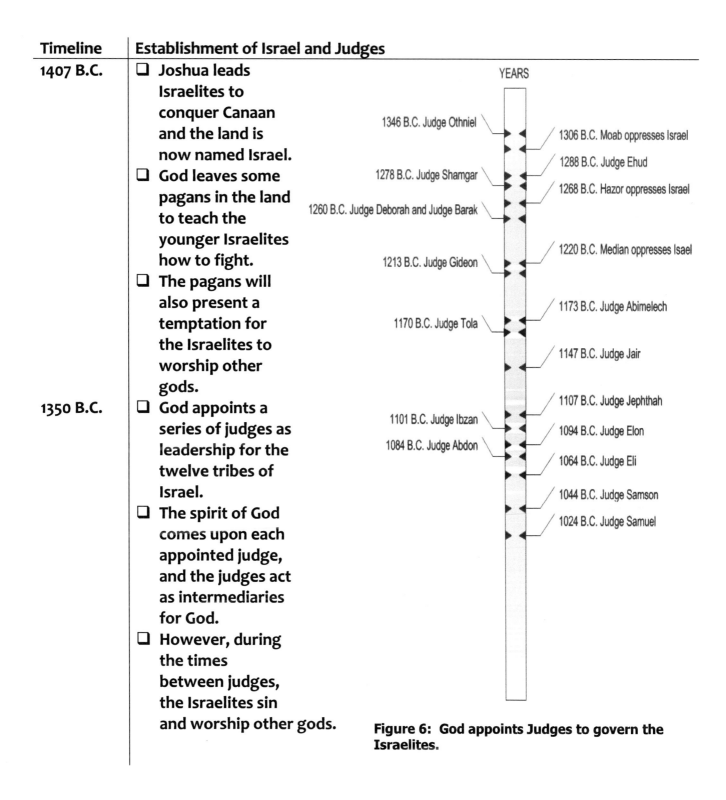

YEARS

1346 B.C. Judge Othniel
1306 B.C. Moab oppresses Israel
1288 B.C. Judge Ehud
1278 B.C. Judge Shamgar
1268 B.C. Hazor oppresses Israel
1260 B.C. Judge Deborah and Judge Barak
1220 B.C. Median oppresses Isael
1213 B.C. Judge Gideon
1173 B.C. Judge Abimelech
1170 B.C. Judge Tola
1147 B.C. Judge Jair
1107 B.C. Judge Jephthah
1101 B.C. Judge Ibzan
1094 B.C. Judge Elon
1084 B.C. Judge Abdon
1064 B.C. Judge Eli
1044 B.C. Judge Samson
1024 B.C. Judge Samuel

Figure 6: God appoints Judges to govern the Israelites.

Timeline	Kings
	❑ Jealous of the surrounding wealthier nations, the Israelites request a king to replace the judges.
	❑ God anoints the kings, but God speaks through prophets.
	❑ The Prophet Greater than Moses will be known as the Anointed One, or Messiah.
1051 B.C.	❑ The first King is Saul, anointed by the last Judge and first Prophet, Samuel.
	❑ God took King Saul's kingdom away because he was jealous of David.
1011 B.C.	❑ King David strengthens the interdependence of the twelve tribes of Israel and has a heart for God.
	❑ Prophet Nathan says the House of David will produce the Forever King.
	❑ King David writes in Psalms that the Messiah would be the Son of God, resurrected, despised, crucified, Lord, Forever King.
971 B.C.	❑ The next king, Solomon, replaces the Tabernacle with the First Temple to worship God, and sacrifices are administered by the High Priest in the Temple.
	❑ God maintains a presence in the Holy of Holies, the innermost room of the Temple.
	❑ King Solomon builds Israel's infrastructure, including palaces, roads, and city walls.

HISTORICAL ATLAS OF HOLY LAND 34

PALESTINE
UNDER DAVID AND SOLOMON
ABOUT 1015-930 B.C.

Figure 7: Israel peaks in power and wealth under King Solomon.

Timeline	Separation of the Kingdoms
931 B.C.	❑ Civil war ensues after King Solomon's death. ❑ King Jeroboam separates the northern ten tribes into an independent nation called Israel and sets up a capital city in Samaria. ❑ King Jeroboam sets up idol worship in Samaria to prevent his Israelite constituency from fleeing to Jerusalem to worship God. ❑ King Rehoboam retains a nation consisting only of the southern two tribes, now called Judah, with capital city Jerusalem. Jews worship God in Jerusalem. ❑ All the Northern Israel Kings are evil in the Lord's sight, since they worship other gods in Samaria. ❑ Several Southern Judah Kings follow God and are good. They are Asa, Jehoshaphat, Amaziah, Hezekiah, and Josiah. ❑ However, the other Southern Judah Kings are evil in the Lord's sight, eventually leading the people of Judah to worship other gods.

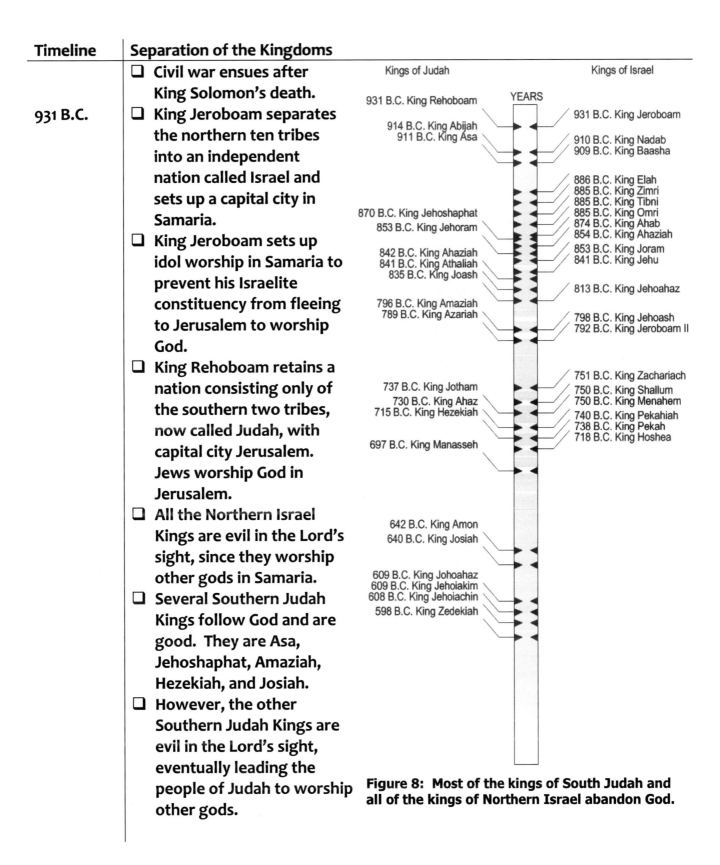

Figure 8: Most of the kings of South Judah and all of the kings of Northern Israel abandon God.

Timeline	Northern Kingdom of Israel and Southern Kingdom of Judah
	❑ Prophets Ahijah, Jehu, Elijah, Micaiah (not to be confused with Micah), Elisha and Amos warn Northern Israel to return to God.
	❑ Prophet Jonah warns pagan Assyria, capital Nineveh, to repent. Assyria repents for a short time, abandoning their multiple gods to worship God.
722 B.C.	❑ Later, however, Assyria returns to idol worship, conquers and carries away much of Northern Israel, then inhabits the land and dominates the remaining Israelites. The Northern ten tribes integrate with pagans, and today's society calls them the "Ten Lost Tribes of Israel."
	❑ Prophet Isaiah prays, and Southern Judah is saved from Assyria by God.
	❑ Prophet Isaiah predicts that the Messiah would: be God and Man; heal the blind, lame, and deaf; be preceded by a forerunner; be a light to the gentiles; be whipped and beaten; die as a guilt offering for sin; and be resurrected to live forever.
	❑ Prophet Micah predicts that the Messiah would be everlasting.
	❑ Prophet Nahum predicts the fall of Assyria.
	❑ Jews of Southern Judah are pridefully confident because they worship in Jerusalem.
	❑ Prophets Zephaniah, Jeremiah, and Habakkuk warn Judah not to be complacent.
586 B.C.	❑ Judah worships other gods, so God allows pagan Babylonians to conquer Southern Judah.
	❑ The leaders and skilled population of Southern Judah are exiled to Babylon. The poor remain to tend to the land.
	❑ The First Temple, Solomon's Temple, is destroyed.
	❑ Prophet Jeremiah predicts the exile will last for 70 years.
	❑ Prophet Jeremiah predicts the Messiah would be God and a righteous Branch.
	❑ Prophet Habakkuk predicts that the Messiah would return full of glory.

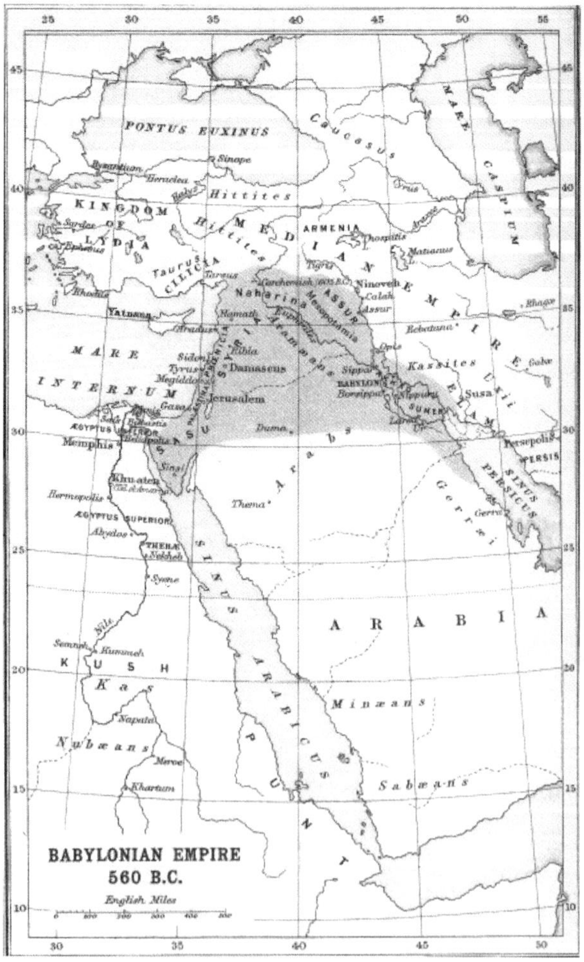

Figure 9: God allows Babylon to conquer Judah and exile the Jews.

Timeline	Babylonian Exile and Return to Jerusalem
	❑ Babylonia is a large, wealthy kingdom. The Hanging Gardens of Babylon are one of the Seven Wonders of the Ancient World. Babylonia's pagan rituals trouble the hearts of Jews, who mourn for their own land.
	❑ Jews in Babylon use a revised Hebrew language largely consisting of Aramaic and Akkadian influences.
	❑ Prophets Ezekiel and Daniel encourage Jews while in Babylon.
	❑ Prophet Ezekiel foretells that the Messiah would be a descendant of David.
	❑ Prophet Daniel predicts that the Messiah would be given an everlasting kingdom.
	❑ Prophet Daniel reads Jeremiah's prophecy that the Jews would return to Jerusalem after 70 years and prays for the Jews.
538 B.C.	❑ God allows Media-Persia to conquer Babylonia and territories.
	❑ Kings of the Persians and the Medes send Jews back to Jerusalem to worship God.
	❑ Prophet Haggai predicts that the Messiah would visit a Second Temple that had not yet been planned since the first temple was destroyed.
	❑ Prophet Zechariah predicts that the Messiah would be Priest and King; would ride into Jerusalem on a donkey; would be God; and would be pierced.

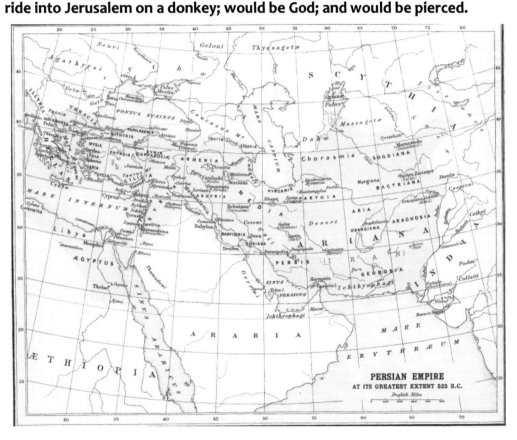

Figure 10: God prompts Persian and Median kings to permit the Jews to return to Jerusalem.

Timeline	Jews rebuild the Temple
536 B.C.	❑ Prophets Ezra and Nehemiah encourage returning Jews to rebuild the Jerusalem City walls and a Second Temple. ❑ Returning Jews are poor, and the Second Temple starts out humble. ❑ Temple Leaders make sure that Jews never again worship false gods by setting up rituals and regulations around God's Laws. ❑ Sacrifices are re-introduced by the High Priest in the Second Temple. ❑ Prophet Malachi predicts that the Messiah would appear at the Temple and that the Messiah's forerunner would come in the spirit of Elijah.
430 B.C.	❑ The prophets complete the books of the Old Testament. ❑ The Abrahamic Covenant is fulfilled, since the nation of Israel is back in the promised land and they are worshiping God. ❑ However, the Messiah that the Prophets have promised has not been revealed.

Figure 11: Jews rebuild the Temple.

Timeline	Rise of the Greek and Roman Empires
	❑ There are 400 years of silence, where no prophets are sent, between the Old and New Testaments.
332 B.C.	❑ Alexander the Great conquers the territories of Media-Persia, including Jerusalem.
	❑ Altars to Greek gods are set up in the Temple in Jerusalem. A small group of Jews called the Maccabees are able to take back control of the Temple, rededicating the Temple to God. The Dedication of the Temple is introduced as an annual holiday.
	❑ Greeks install local governors for the territory of Israel.
	❑ Greek culture and language are used, even after this territory was overtaken by the Romans.
63 B.C.	❑ Greeks used the Romans as their military, but eventually the Romans take over control of the territories.
	❑ Romans continue to use the Greek language, as well as Latin.
	❑ Early Roman Emperors allow the Jews to practice their religion, but set up local governors.
	❑ Jews are heavily taxed by local tax collectors as well as their Roman rulers.

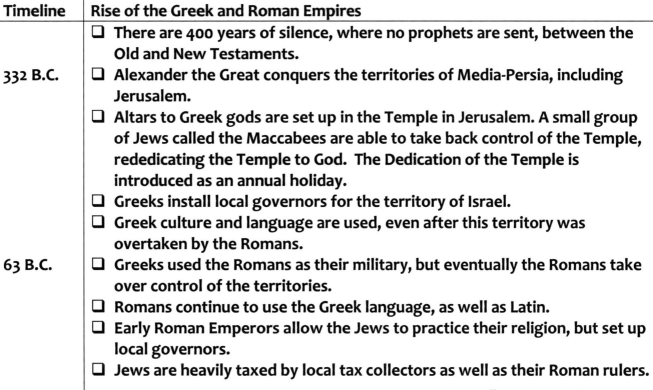

HISTORICAL ATLAS OF HOLY LAND

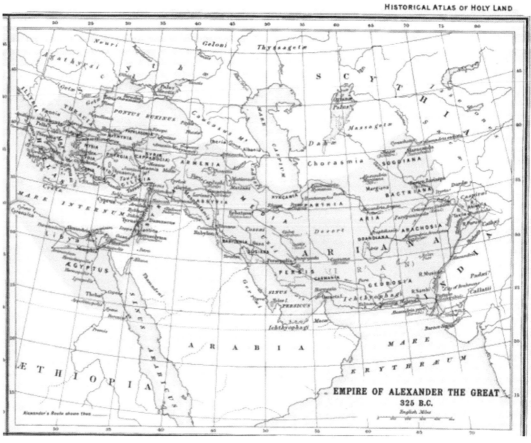

EMPIRE OF ALEXANDER THE GREAT
325 B.C.

Figure 12: Jews maintain limited control of Jerusalem and the Temple under the Greek Empire (displayed) and Roman Empire (figure 14).

Timeline	Jesus' Ministry
3 B.C.	❑ The New Testament begins with the Nativity, which are miracles surrounding the birth of Jesus.
26 A.D.	❑ John the Baptist announces that the Messiah is coming soon.
27 A.D.	❑ Jesus' earthly ministry is during Roman rule of Jerusalem.
	❑ People recognize Jesus as the Messiah because (1) Jesus fulfills the Prophets' predictions concerning Him; (2) Jesus performs miracles of healing, teaching, and knowledge of future events; and (3) Jesus says He's the Messiah.
	❑ The local Jewish Leaders, the Pharisees and the Sadducees, consider Jesus a threat to their leadership and do not recognize Jesus as the Messiah.

Figure 13: Jesus is born under miraculous circumstances. Jesus fulfills all the Messianic predictions of the prophets.

❑ Jesus is most critical of the local Jewish Leaders, Pharisees and Sadducees, who pretend to be pious, rather than Israel's cruel Roman rulers.

❑ Jesus chooses twelve devoted students, called Disciples, to accompany him.

❑ Jewish leaders accuse Jesus of heresy and arrange punishment of death by hanging him on a wooden cross, called a crucifix.

❑ Jesus is crucified. In fear, the Disciples abandon Jesus.

30 A.D.

❑ The body of Jesus is buried in a tomb, and then is resurrected back to life on the third day after the crucifixion.

❑ Jesus appears to His Disciples. The Holy Spirit descends on each Disciple. The Disciples transform into brave men carrying the good news of Jesus' resurrection. The Disciples are now Apostles, or messengers.

❑ Jesus is seen by hundreds in His glorified, resurrected state as the Holy Spirit moves freely among the believers.

❑ Jesus ascends to Heaven, leaving those who believe in Jesus as the Messiah with the gift of the Holy Spirit, as well as protection from evil.

❑ Apostles and other Believers start churches.

❑ Jesus leaves evil here on Earth, for a time, to teach people how to be spiritually strong and become overcomers of the world and their fleshly base nature.

Timeline	Christianity
70 A.D.	❑ Jews revolt when Roman Caesar Caligula sets up statues of himself in the Second Temple.
	❑ Roman Legions destroy the Second Temple.
	❑ Temple sacrifices halt when the Second Temple is destroyed.
	❑ Jesus' Disciples and Apostles teach the New Covenant and Perfect Sacrifice, which is that Jesus is Forever High Priest, Jesus is the Forever Perfect Sacrifice, and the Temple resides thereafter in the Hearts of Believers.
95 A.D.	❑ Jesus' Disciples and Apostles complete the books of the New Testament, including Prophecy of events still to come.
	❑ Christianity spreads throughout the world based on (1) the testimony, or narrative, of the Disciples who know Jesus personally; (2) the corroboration of the Disciples' testimony by secular historians and other professionals; and (3) the inexplicable kindness and compassion demonstrated by Believers.

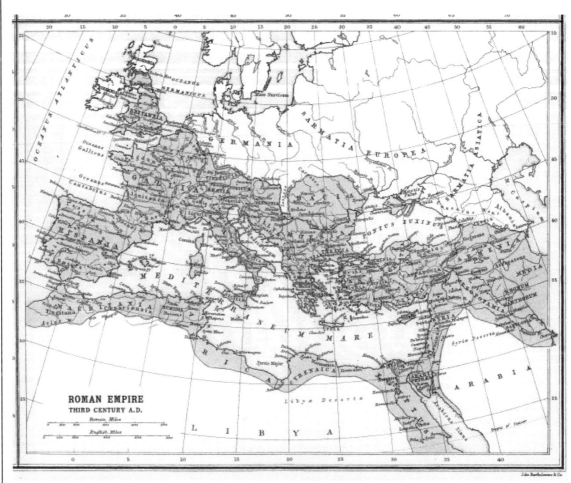

Figure 14: The Roman Empire was responsible for the destruction of the Second Temple as Jesus foretold.

Study this Book of Instruction continually. Meditate on it day and night so you will be sure to obey everything written in it. Only then will you prosper and succeed in all you do.

                                                                    —Joshua 1:8

SUMMARY OF THE BOOKS OF THE BIBLE

This chapter explains how the books of the common Christian Bible are organized.

	Summary of the Old and New Testaments
	❑ The 66 books of the Bible are divided into two main sections: the Old Testament, with 39 books, and the New Testament, with 27 books.
	❑ Each book of the Bible is further segmented into chapters, and each chapter is divided into verses.
430 B.C.	❑ The books of the Old Testament are originally written in Hebrew, the language of the Israelites, with occasional Akkadian/Aramaic influences.
	❑ There are 4 sections of the Old Testament:
	○ (1) Pentateuch, the first 5 books of Moses, from Genesis through Deuteronomy, explaining God's perfect Creation through the Israelites return from Egypt.
	○ (2) Old Testament History, from Joshua through Esther, runs chronologically from the establishment of Israel to the Israelite return from Babylonian exile.
	○ (3) Old Testament Poetry, from Job through Song of Songs, includes Israelite folklore, song books, and sayings.
	○ (4) Old Testament Prophets, from Isaiah through Malachi, are not in chronological order. Major Prophets are first, Isaiah through Daniel, called major because their books are longer. Minor Prophets are second, Hosea through Malachi, called minor because their books are shorter. The Prophets guide, warn, and encourage the Israelites during the period of the Kings as well as after their return from exile in Babylon.
95 A.D.	❑ The books of the New Testament are originally written in Greek by Jesus' Disciples and Apostles.
	❑ There are 4 sections of the New Testament:
	○ (1) New Testament Gospels, from Matthew through John, each contain the same story of Jesus Christ, but addressed to different audiences.
	○ (2) New Testament History, Acts, includes the story of the Churches.
	○ (3) New Testament Churches, from Romans through Jude, includes Letters written to the Churches by the Disciples and Apostles.
	○ (4) New Testament Revelation, which includes prophesy of events still to come.

In the beginning was the Word, and the Word was with God, and the Word was God.

--John 1:1

BOOKS OF THE BIBLE

This chapter identifies the author of each book of the Bible and how each book fits into the overall plot. They are listed in the order in which they appear in the Bible.

Timeline	Old Testament Pentateuch
1445 B.C.	❑ Moses writes the first 5 books, Genesis to Deuteronomy, mostly while the Israelites wandered in the desert for 40 years. ❑ Genesis recounts history from God's perfect creation and the Fall (sin) to the establishment of the Israelite people from Abraham, Isaac, Jacob (Israel) and the twelve tribes migrating to Egypt.
1406 B.C.	❑ Exodus recounts history from the Israelite escape from Egypt to migration back to Canaan. ❑ Leviticus explains the Laws that God establishes for the Israelites. ❑ Numbers covers the census of families in the Israelite community. ❑ Deuteronomy is a summary of Genesis and Exodus. Moses reviews history with the Israelites in preparation for entry into Canaan.

Figure 15: Moses breaks the Ten Commandments in response to Israelite disobedience.

Timeline	Old Testament History
1375 B.C.	❑ Joshua writes most of the book of Joshua, which tells how the Israelites conquer Canaan and rename the land Israel.
1050 B.C.	❑ Prophet Samuel writes the tail end of the book of Joshua, as well as Judges and Ruth. Judges recounts each judge that God sends to govern Israel. Ruth is a love story set during the time of the judges.
970 B.C.	❑ Prophet Samuel writes 1 Samuel, which explains the transition from judges to kings in Israel, as well as from the anointing to the death of the first king, King Saul.
930 B.C.	❑ Prophet Isaiah writes 2 Samuel, which explains the unification of Israel under King David.
560 B.C.	❑ Prophet Isaiah compiles 1 Kings and 2 Kings, which starts with King Solomon and the establishment of the Temple, through Assyria conquering the Northern Tribes of Israel and Babylon conquering the Southern Tribes of Judah. The history is originally recorded primarily by Prophet Elijah.
430 B.C.	❑ Prophet Ezra compiles 1 Chronicles and 2 Chronicles, and writes Ezra. Chronicles 1 and 2 are a summary of Genesis through 2 Kings to prepare the Israelites to return to Jerusalem from their exile in Babylon. Ezra talks about the first wave of Jews that return to Jerusalem from Babylon. Prophet Nehemiah writes Nehemiah, which talks about the second wave of Jews that return to Jerusalem after Media-Persia conquers Babylon.
470 B.C.	❑ Prophet Ezra also writes Esther, the details of a Jewish woman in the foreign land of Media-Persia who saves the Jewish population.

Figure 16: Prophet Samuel blesses the first king, King Saul.

Timeline	Old Testament Poetry
1800 B.C.	❑ Job is written by Job and is mostly poetry as Job and his friends spiritually and emotionally work through a series of disasters.
1440 B.C. to 586 B.C.	❑ Psalms is the Israelite song book. The songs are written by Moses, King David, and King Solomon, as well as Temple musicians Asaph, Sons of Korah, Heman, Ethan the Ezrahite, and other unidentified lyricists.
930 B.C.	❑ King Solomon writes Proverbs, a book of sayings; Ecclesiastes, a book of advice; and Song of Songs, a love story.

Figure 17: Job hears of his ruin.

Timeline	Old Testament Prophets
	Major Prophets:
680 B.C.	❏ Isaiah - Isaiah writes when Assyria conquers Northern Israel, and warns Southern Judah not to follow in Israel's footsteps or she'll be conquered as well.
586 B.C.	❏ Jeremiah - Jeremiah warns Judah of the coming Babylonians, predicting that Babylonia will conquer Judah, but that after 70 years, Jews would return to rebuild Jerusalem. Jeremiah writes Lamentations during the Babylonian exile.
570 B.C.	❏ **Ezekiel - Ezekiel and Jeremiah are contemporaries. Ezekiel also warns Judah of the Babylonians and is exiled to Babylon.**
535 B.C.	❏ **Daniel - Daniel is a young man when he is exiled to Babylon. He rises to importance in Babylon. He prays for the Jews when reading in Jeremiah that the 70 years of exile have passed.**

Figure 18: Prophet Daniel is exiled to Babylon as a young man, along with most of the Jewish leadership, while only the poor are left in Israel to tend to the land.

Timeline	Old Testament Prophets
	Minor Prophets:
715 B.C.	❑ **Hosea** - Hosea writes before North Israel is captured by the Assyrians. His message is a warning about abandoning God.
800 B.C.	❑ **Joel** - Joel writes about a plague of locusts and a severe drought, referencing the future destruction of Israel.
750 B.C.	❑ **Amos** - Amos preaches when Northern Israel is wealthy, warning the Israelites about sins concerning greed and corruption.
845 B.C.	❑ **Obadiah** - Obadiah predicts the destruction of Edom, a country to the south, because Edom took advantage of the Israelites when they were returning to Canaan from Egypt.
760 B.C.	❑ **Jonah** - Jonah warns Assyrians to repent 75 years before Assyrians conquer Northern Israel.
687 B.C.	❑ **Micah** - Micah explains that Northern Israel is captured by Assyria due to idolatry and greed. Micah foresees Jewish exile and subsequent return of a remnant of the Jewish population.
612 B.C.	❑ **Nahum** - Nahum witnesses the Babylonian invasion of Southern Judah. He prophesizes that Babylon would be conquered. Nahum, Habakkuk, and Zephaniah are contemporaries.
589 B.C.	❑ **Habakkuk** - Habakkuk explains that the Babylonian invasion is intended to punish Southern Judah.
621 B.C.	❑ **Zephaniah** - Zephaniah predicts the destruction of the Babylonian empire.
520 B.C.	❑ **Haggai** - Haggai encourages the Israelites returning from Babylonian exile to rebuild the Temple in Jerusalem. Haggai and Zechariah are contemporaries.
480 B.C.	❑ **Zechariah** - Zechariah encourages the Israelites returning from Babylonian exile to purify the Temple in Jerusalem.
420 B.C.	❑ **Malachi** – Not long after the Temple is rebuilt following the Babylonian exile, Malachi warns the Jewish priests that they are being lax in their commitment to God.

Figure 19: Prophet Micah warns the population of Southern Judah of the danger of greed and corruption.

Timeline	New Testament Gospels
	❑ Gospel means good news. Each book is about the life of Jesus and bears the name of the author.
	❑ Matthew, Mark, Luke and John are followers of Jesus.
65 A.D.	❑ Matthew, a Jewish tax collector for Rome who was a disciple of Jesus, writes the complete story to Jewish readers, from Jesus' birth to resurrection, and includes genealogy, miracles, teachings, and messianic prophecy.
65 A.D.	❑ Mark, a younger man, writes a shorter story to gentiles (i.e. non-Jewish readers), and includes miracles, teachings, and salvation.
60 A.D.	❑ Luke, a physician, writes a full investigative report to an official, and includes genealogy, birth, teachings, miracles, predictions, the resurrection, as well as history and geography.
90 A.D.	❑ John, a disciple of Jesus, writes a spiritual account of Jesus' ministry, mostly the unseen side of the story with a focus on the spiritual realm.

Figure 20: Jesus preaches to the crowd. Later, His Disciples compile the sermons into their gospels.

Timeline	New Testament History

70 A.D.

❑ Acts, written by the physician Luke, provides the account of the Disciples and Apostles after Jesus' resurrection. Although cowardly during the crucifixion of Jesus, the Disciples transform into courageous men able to work miracles after the Holy Spirit indwells them. The Disciples and Apostles of Jesus launch the Church, which is the name for the assembly of all Believers. Individual churches, or places where Believers gather, are also started.

Figure 21: The Holy Spirit descends on the Disciples, empowering them with testimony and miracles.

Timeline	New Testament Churches
	❑ Paul, an apostle, writes many New Testament letters to Christians in different cities:
57 A.D.	o **Romans** - Christian faith and salvation.
55 A.D.	o **1 Corinthians** - Spiritual gifts and the meaning of the resurrection.
56 A.D.	o **2 Corinthians** - Endurance in the service of Christ.
48 A.D.	o **Galatians** – Freedom in Christ.
60 A.D.	o **Ephesians** – Spirit-guided relationships and spiritual protection.
60 A.D.	o **Philippians** – The Joy of Christ.
60 A.D.	o **Colossians** - The Lordship of Christ.
51 A.D	o **1 Thessalonians** – The hope of the resurrection.
	o **2 Thessalonians** – Preparing Believers for the return of Christ.
63 A.D.	o **1 Timothy** - Duties of Church officers.
	o **2 Timothy** – Qualification of Church officers.
64 A.D.	o **Titus** - Addresses problems of a young minister.
60 A.D.	o **Philemon** - Personal letter asking for mercy for a runaway slave.
70 A.D.	o **Hebrews** - Definition of faith and Jesus as High Priest and Perfect Sacrifice. Authorship of this book is not always thought to be Paul.
49 A.D.	❑ James, a disciple, writes the book of James about Christian ethics.
67 A.D.	❑ Peter, a disciple, writes 1 Peter and 2 Peter about persecution, suffering, and faithfulness.
90 A.D.	❑ John, a disciple, writes 1 John, 2 John, and 3 John about eternal life and hospitality. He also wrote Revelation, as well as the Gospel book of John.
70 A.D.	❑ Jude, a disciple, writes Jude about the dangers of corruption.

Figure 22: Apostle Paul preaches to the members of the Thessalonian Church.

Timeline	New Testament Revelation
95 A.D.	❑ John, the disciple who wrote the Gospel of John and John 1, 2, and 3, later writes the Revelation. Revelation addresses shortcomings of the members of seven churches and prophesizes about events leading up to the ultimate victory of Christ against Satan. There is disagreement as to the date it was written.

Figure 23: John, a beloved Disciple of Jesus, sees the New Jerusalem, part of prophesy yet to come.

Heaven and earth will disappear, but my words will never disappear.

—Matthew 24:35

HISTORY OF THE WRITTEN WORD

This chapter explains how the manuscripts of the Bible progress from their origins as scrolls in the desert to today's published volume.

Timeline	Five Books of Moses
1400 B.C.	❑ Moses writes Genesis, Exodus, Leviticus, Numbers, and Deuteronomy while the Israelites wander for 40 years in the desert on the way back from their slavery in Egypt. ❑ God gives the Ten Commandments to Moses at Mount Sinai. ❑ Moses writes using ancient Hebrew on scrolls made from animal skins.

Figure 24: Moses descends from Mount Sinai with Ten Commandments from God.

Timeline	Old Testament Manuscripts
400 B.C.	❑ The first 5 books are the books of Moses, also known as the Pentateuch. Joshua writes the Book of Joshua. ❑ Prophet Samuel writes Judges, Ruth, and 1 Samuel. ❑ Prophet Isaiah compiles 2 Samuel, 1 Kings, and 2 Kings. ❑ Prophet Ezra compiles 1 Chronicles, 2 Chronicles, Ezra, and Esther. ❑ Prophet Nehemiah writes the book of Nehemiah. ❑ Moses, King David, and King Solomon, as well as Temple musicians Asaph, Sons of Korah, Heman, Ethan the Ezrahite, and other unidentified lyricists contribute to the Psalms songbook. **Figure 25: King Solomon writes poetry and advice, later compiled into the books of Proverbs, Ecclesiastes, and Song of Songs.** ❑ Job writes the book of Job. ❑ King Solomon writes Proverbs, Ecclesiastes, and Song of Songs of Solomon. ❑ Prophets Isaiah, Jeremiah, Ezekiel, Daniel, Hosea, Joel, Obadiah, Jonah, Micah, Nahum, Habakkuk, Zephaniah, Haggai, Zechariah, and Malachi write books bearing their names. ❑ The 39 Old Testament Manuscripts are written in ancient Hebrew on scrolls made from animal skins

Timeline	Septuagint
250 B.C.	❏ The Hebrew Manuscripts are translated into Greek, called the Septuagint. ❏ Manuscripts contain 39 Old Testament books and 14 Apocryphal books. ❏ Apocrypha means "secret." These books are in a separate section with names like "The Book of Baruch", "The Wisdom of Solomon", and "The Prayer of Manasseh." The authors of the apocryphal books are uncertain but use the names of biblical men for their pen names. The Septuagint is written on papyrus, a paper-like material made from flattened stalks of a reed-like plant. The papyrus sheets are tied together like a book, called a codex. ❏ The five books of Moses written on papyrus are called the Pentateuch.

Figure 26: Baruch is Prophet Jeremiah's Secretary. However, the author of the Book of Baruch is unknown.

Timeline	New Testament Manuscripts
95 A.D.	❑ Disciples Matthew and John, along with Mark (a follower of Disciple Peter) and Physician Luke, write Gospels, which means "good news." ❑ Apostle Paul and Disciples James, Peter, and Jude write letters to the Churches and individuals. ❑ Disciple John, author of the Gospel of John, also writes letters to Churches, as well as prophecy still to come. ❑ The 27 books of the New Testament are written in Greek on papyrus

Figure 27: John, a beloved Disciple of Jesus, writes the book of the Revelation, including prophecy still to come, while imprisoned on the Island of Patmos.

Timeline	Canon of Scripture
367 A.D.	❑ Athenasius, the Bishop of Alexandria, identifies the 27 books of the New Testament upon which Christians universally agree as the minimal Christian canon of scripture. Some Christian churches include additional books known as Apocrypha which are recognized by them as canon (i.e. the accepted word of God).
382 A.D.	❑ The Roman Catholic Church commissions Jerome's Latin Vulgate Manuscripts to include 80 books: 39 Old Testament, 27 New Testament, and 14 Apocrypha. The Apocrypha is kept in a separate section due to a lack of consensus regarding the inerrancy or authorship of each books.
500 A.D.	❑ The Septuagint is the basis for Bible translations into Latin and Gothic in the West, and Syriac, Coptic, Armenian, Georgian, Ethiopic, and Sogdian in the East.
600 A.D.	❑ Vellum, a fine parchment made from calf skin is used by Bible scribes. ❑ Documents are written in rag-paper made from cotton, linen, and other vegetable fibers. ❑ The Bible is labor intensive to reproduce and few people other than priests and churches have the Bible available to study. Believers have little access to the Bible except as presented by the priests, and there are sporadic movements to help bring the word to believers in additional translations, but no movements are very successful for many centuries.

Figure 28: York Minster Cathedral, York, United Kingdom, circa 1100 A.D., is built during the European Middle Ages.

Timeline	Protestant Reformation
1300 A.D.	❑ Christian Reformation begins where champions arise to get the Word of God into the hands of the masses.
1384 A.D.	❑ John Wycliffe is the first person to translate and produce a hand-written manuscript copy of the complete Bible from Latin into English; all 80 books. Wycliffe helped initiate the Protestant Reformation to reintroduce the Bible to the people in their native languages.
1415 A.D.	❑ Paper is made from beating wood, straw, and cloth into a fine pulp, mixing with water, and then sheets of paper are pressed out, dried, and hardened.

Figure 29: John Wycliffe produces the first English language Bible.

Timeline	Mass Publication
1455 A.D.	❏ Johannes Gutenberg invents the printing press. Books may now be mass-produced instead of individually hand-written. The first book ever printed is Gutenberg's Bible in Latin.
1516 A.D.	❏ Erasmus (aka St. Elmo) produces a Greek/Latin Parallel New Testament using original Greek and Hebrew manuscripts for increased accuracy.
1517 A.D.	❏ Martin Luther nails his famous 95 Theses of protest to the door of the Roman Catholic church at Wittenberg, Germany, thereby hastening the Protestant Reformation that would establish the priesthood of all believers, make the Bible available to everybody, and challenge church doctrines.
1522 A.D.	❏ Martin Luther publishes the New Testament in German.
1526 A.D.	❏ William Tyndale publishes the New Testament in the English Language.
1535 A.D.	❏ Myles Coverdale publishes the first complete Bible printed in the English Language, including 80 books: Old Testament, New Testament, and a separate section for Apocrypha.
1537 A.D.	❏ The second complete Bible printed in English is the Tyndale-Matthew Bible by John "Thomas Matthew" Rogers, including 80 books.
1539 A.D.	❏ King Henry VIII allows and funds the printing of an English Bible called the "Great Bible", the first English language Bible authorized for public use, including 80 books. King Henry VIII's motives for doing so are partially selfish. He desires to divorce his wife and marry his mistress, which is not allowed by the Roman Catholic Church. So, King Henry VIII renounces Roman Catholicism and starts the Anglican Church which allows for divorce, and publishes the English-language Great Bible.

Figure 30: Portrait of King Henry VIII in early manhood by an unknown artist. King Henry VIII published the Great Bible.

Timeline	The King James Bible
1542 A.D.	❑ The Roman Catholic Council of Trent is a meeting of church leaders who attempt to reunify the church in response to the blossoming Protestant Reformation. The Council decides to reaffirm the Apocryphal books into the Old Testament canon of the Roman Catholic Church, thus elevating these writings to have a status of inerrancy within the Roman Catholic Church and thus validating church doctrines that only appear in apocryphal books.
1560 A.D.	❑ The Geneva Bible is a result of Protestant scholars meeting on neutral ground to produce an English Bible from original languages. This is the first English language Bible to assign chapter and verse numbers to the text. The Geneva Bible typically consisted of 80 books, with apocrypha isolated into a separate section between the Old and New Testament.
1568 A.D.	❑ The Bishops Bible is printed. The King James is a revision of the Bishops Bible (80 books with apocrypha in a separate section).
1609 A.D.	❑ The Catholic Bible is the first English translation of the Catholic's Latin Bible, derived from Douay Old Testament and the Rheims New Testament of 1582, both of which were translated from the Latin Vulgate. This 80 book Catholic Bible also integrated the Apocrypha as part of the Old Testament canon.
1611 A.D.	❑ The King James Bible, also known as the Authorized Version, is printed, originally with 80 books (with apocrypha) by the order of King James of England in 1604.

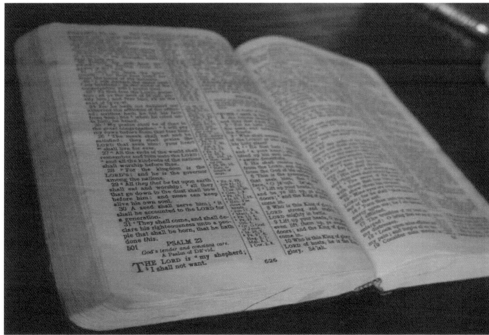

Figure 31: This King James Version (KJV) Bible is open at Psalm 23. The King James Version remains an influential and popular translation today.

Timeline	Modern Translations and Study Bibles
1769 A.D.	❑ The Baskerville spelling and wording revision of the 1611 King James Version is printed. For 200 years, the primary KJV available in America is the Baskerville revision.
1782 A.D.	❑ The first English language KJV Bible printed in America is the Robert Aitken's Bible.
1791 A.D.	❑ Isaac Collins and Isaiah Thomas respectively produce the first family Bible and first illustrated Bible printed in America; both King James Versions including 80 books.
1833 A.D.	❑ After producing his famous dictionary, Noah Webster prints his own revision of the King James Bible.
	❑ Paper production improves with the introduction of wood pulp.
1841 A.D.	❑ An early textual comparison showing the Greek and six English translations in parallel columns, called English Hexapla New Testament, is published.
1846 A.D.	❑ The Illuminated Bible, a lavishly illustrated King James Version of the Bible, is printed in America with all 80 books (with apocrypha).
1885 A.D.	❑ The "English Revised Version" Bible is printed, which is the first major English revision of the KJV. The Apocrypha is officially removed, leaving 66 books in the Bible that are accepted canon among Christians internationally, even though the apocrypha continues in many Bibles in various forms.
1901 A.D.	❑ The "American Standard Version" Bible is printer, which is the first major American revision of the KJV.
1971 A.D.	❑ The "New American Standard Bible" (NASB) is published as a "modern and accurate word for word English translation" of the Bible.
1973 A.D.	❑ The "New International Version" (NIV) is published as a "modern and accurate phrase for phrase English translation" of the Bible.
1982 A.D.	❑ The "New King James Version" (NKJV) is published as a "modern English version maintaining the original style of the King James."
1996 A.D.	❑ The "New Living Translation" (NLT) is published using the thought-for-thought method of translation, rather than word-for-word.
2013 A.D.	❑ Portions of the Bible have been translated into over 2,500 of the estimated 6,500 world languages, including 680 in Africa, 590 in Asia, 420 in Oceania, 420 in Latin America and the Caribbean, 210 in Europe, and 75 in North America. The United Bible Societies lists over 600 Bible translation projects in progress.

Such things were written in the Scriptures long ago to teach us. And the Scriptures give us hope and encouragement as we wait patiently for God's promises to be fulfilled.

                                                            –Romans 15:4

The Bible is God's Word for all people for all time. This chapter, Messages of the Bible, contains a sample of the communication that God presents through the Bible. Bible action takes place in Ancient Israel. Understanding the historical setting is necessary in order to translate God's Word into meaningful messages for people in modern day. Israelite leaders, priests, and prophets spoke the messages in the Bible. Bible references are displayed by book, chapter, and verse.

Timeline	Message to the obedient
1991 B.C.	God provides a blessing to the obedient when God calls Abraham into service. Abraham: The LORD had said to Abram, "Leave your native country, your relatives, and your father's family, and go to the land that I will show you. I will make you into a great nation. I will bless you and make you famous, and you will be a blessing to others. I will bless those who bless you and curse those who treat you with contempt. All the families on earth will be blessed through you." [Genesis 12:1-3]

Figure 32: God tests Abraham's faith by asking him to sacrifice his son, Isaac. God substitutes a ram for the sacrifice when Abraham proves faithful.

Then the angel of the LORD called again to Abraham from heaven. "This is what the LORD says: Because you have obeyed me and have not withheld even your son, your only son, I swear by my own name that I will certainly bless you. I will multiply your descendants beyond number, like the stars in the sky and the sand on the seashore. Your descendants will conquer the cities of their enemies. And through your descendants all the nations of the earth will be blessed—all because you have obeyed me." [Genesis 22:15-18]

Timeline	Messages to the enslaved
	As the Israelites return to the promised land of Canaan from slavery in Egypt, Moses reminds them that God is the One who sets the captives free. Later, as the Israelites brave battle to conquer Canaan, Joshua reminds them that God provides the land of Canaan as part of the Covenant to worship only God.
1406 B.C.	**Moses:** At the mountain the LORD spoke to you face to face from the heart of the fire. I stood as an intermediary between you and the LORD, for you were afraid of the fire and did not want to approach the mountain. He spoke to me, and I passed his words on to you. This is what he said: "I am the LORD your God, who rescued you from the land of Egypt, the place of your slavery." [Deuteronomy 5:4-6]
1350 B.C.	**Joshua:** "Soon I will die, going the way of everything on earth. Deep in your hearts you know that every promise of the LORD your God has come true. Not a single one has failed! But as surely as the LORD your God has given you the good things he promised, he will also bring disaster on you if you disobey him. He will completely destroy you from this good land he has given you. If you break the covenant of the LORD your God by worshiping and serving other gods, his anger will burn against you, and you will quickly vanish from the good land he has given you." [Joshua 23:14-16]

Figure 33: Joshua leads the Israelite troops conquering Canaan.

Timeline	Messages to those in battle
	As the Israelites continue to overcome Canaanites, Judge Deborah and Judge Samuel remind them to be faithful to God so that God can provide them with victory.
1144 B.C.	**Deborah:** Then Deborah said to Barak, "Get ready! This is the day the LORD will give you victory over Sisera, for the LORD is marching ahead of you." So Barak led his 10,000 warriors down the slopes of Mount Tabor into battle. [Judges 4:14]
1064 B.C.	**Samuel:** Then Samuel said to all the people of Israel, "If you are really serious about wanting to return to the LORD, get rid of your foreign gods and your images of Ashtoreth. Determine to obey only the LORD; then he will rescue you from the Philistines." [1 Samuel 7:3]

Figure 34: Judge Deborah encourages the Israelites gaining victory in the promised land.

Timeline	Messages to the irresponsible
	As a result of envy, the Israelites ask for a king to replace God's appointed judges, and Judge Samuel is re-assigned to Prophet. Prophet Samuel reprimands the Israelites, but continues to pray for them. Later, King David commits a serious transgression and Prophet Nathan rebukes him.
1004 B.C.	**Samuel:** "As for me, I will certainly not sin against the LORD by ending my prayers for you. And I will continue to teach you what is good and right. But be sure to fear the LORD and faithfully serve him. Think of all the wonderful things he has done for you. But if you continue to sin, you and your king will be swept away." [1 Samuel 12:23-25]
964 B.C.	**Nathan:** Then Nathan said to David, "You are that man! The LORD, the God of Israel, says: I anointed you king of Israel and saved you from the power of Saul. I gave you your master's house and his wives and the kingdoms of Israel and Judah. And if that had not been enough, I would have given you much, much more. Why, then, have you despised the word of the LORD and done this horrible deed? For you have murdered Uriah the Hittite with the sword of the Ammonites and stolen his wife. From this time on, your family will live by the sword because you have despised me by taking Uriah's wife to be your own." [2 Samuel 12:7-10]  **Figure 35: King David's family is plagued with violence due to King David's sin.**

Timeline	Messages to the guilty
	When the Ten Northern Tribes secede, creating the kingdom of Israel and leaving only Two Tribes in the southern kingdom of Judah, the Prophets listed below condemn Northern Israel and predict her destruction, even while the presence of those Prophets demonstrates God's compassion towards the Israelites.

909 B.C.

Ahijah:
He (God) will abandon Israel because Jeroboam sinned and made Israel sin along with him. [1 Kings 14:16]

860 B.C.

Elijah:
At the usual time for offering the evening sacrifice, Elijah the prophet walked up to the altar and prayed, "O LORD, God of Abraham, Isaac, and Jacob, prove today that you are God in Israel and that I am your servant.
Prove that I have done all this at your command." [1 Kings 18:36]

Figure 36: God works miracles through Prophet Elijah. God sends prophets to both Northern Israel and Southern Judah as well as to pagan nations.

851 B.C.

Elisha:
But when Elisha, the man of God, heard that the king of Israel had torn his clothes in dismay, he sent this message to him: "Why are you so upset? Send Naaman to me, and he will learn that there is a true prophet here in Israel." [2 Kings 5:8]

741 B.C.

Hosea:
When the LORD first began speaking to Israel through Hosea, he said to him, "Go and marry a prostitute, so that some of her children will be conceived in prostitution. This will illustrate how Israel has acted like a prostitute by turning against the LORD and worshiping other gods." [Hosea 1:2]

715 B.C.

Isaiah:
"Then the LORD will bring things on you, your nation, and your family unlike anything since Israel broke away from Judah. He will bring the king of Assyria upon you!" [Isaiah 7:17]

Timeline	Messages during punishment
	Prophets remind the Israelites that, even through a disaster of the Israelites own making, God intends to forgive and bless them.
795 B.C.	Joel: The LORD says, "I will give you back what you lost to the swarming locusts, the hopping locusts, the stripping locusts, and the cutting locusts. It was I who sent this great destroying army against you. Once again you will have all the food you want, and you will praise the LORD your God, who does these miracles for you. Never again will my people be disgraced. Then you will know that I am among my people Israel, that I am the LORD your God, and there is no other. Never again will my people be disgraced." [Joel 2:25-27]

Figure 37: Prophet Isaiah delivers messages to the Israelites from God.

Timeline	Messages during punishment
715 B.C.	Isaiah: "Come now, let's settle this," says the LORD. "Though your sins are like scarlet, I will make them as white as snow. Though they are red like crimson, I will make them as white as wool." [Isaiah 1:18]

Timeline	Messages to outsiders
	Non-Jews, called gentiles, are pagan, meaning they worship other gods. God calls Jewish Prophets to inform gentile nations that God extends blessings to them as well.
767 B.C.	**Jonah:** This time Jonah obeyed the LORD's command and went to Nineveh, a city so large that it took three days to see it all. On the day Jonah entered the city, he shouted to the crowds: "Forty days from now Nineveh will be destroyed!" The people of Nineveh believed God's message, and from the greatest to the least, they declared a fast and put on burlap to show their sorrow. [Jonah 4:3-5]
715 B.C.	**Isaiah:** "I, the LORD, have called you to demonstrate my righteousness. I will take you by the hand and guard you, and I will give you to my people, Israel, as a symbol of my covenant with them. And you will be a light to guide the nations." [Isaiah 42:6]

Figure 38: Prophet Jonah preaches to the pagan population in Nineveh, capital of Assyria.

Timeline	Messages to the rebellious
	As the southern kingdom of Judah follows the northern kingdom of Israel into disobedience by worshipping other gods, Prophets plea for the people to return to God.

741 B.C.

Amos:
Listen to this message that the LORD has spoken against you, O people of Israel and Judah—against the entire family I rescued from Egypt: "From among all the families on the earth, I have been intimate with you alone. That is why I must punish you for all your sins." [Amos 3:2]

Figure 39: Prophet Amos explains God's discipline to the Israelites.

724 B.C.

Micah:
And why is this happening? Because of the rebellion of Israel — yes, the sins of the whole nation. Who is to blame for Israel's rebellion? Samaria, its capital city! Where is the center of idolatry in Judah? In Jerusalem, its capital! [Micah 1:5]

741 B.C.

Hosea:
"O Israel and Judah, what should I do with you?" asks the LORD. "For your love vanishes like the morning mist and disappears like dew in the sunlight. I sent my prophets to cut you to pieces— to slaughter you with my words, with judgments as inescapable as light. I want you to show love, not offer sacrifices. I want you to know me more than I want burnt offerings. But like Adam, you broke my covenant and betrayed my trust." [Hosea 6:4-7]

Timeline	Messages to the stubborn
	Even after the northern kingdom of Israel is conquered by Assyria, the southern kingdom of Judah refuses to return to God. Prophets predict that Judah will suffer for disobedience, but that eventually Judah's people will repent and return to God.
715 B.C.	**Isaiah:** Then Isaiah said to Hezekiah, "Listen to this message from the LORD: The time is coming when everything in your palace—all the treasures stored up by your ancestors until now—will be carried off to Babylon. Nothing will be left, says the LORD." [2 Kings 20:16-17]
609 B.C.	**Jeremiah:** During the reign of King Josiah, the LORD said to me, "Have you seen what fickle Israel has done? Like a wife who commits adultery, Israel has worshiped other gods on every hill and under every green tree. I thought, 'After she has done all this, she will return to me.' But she did not return, and her faithless sister Judah saw this. She saw that I divorced faithless Israel because of her adultery. But that treacherous sister Judah had no fear, and now she, too, has left me and given herself to prostitution. Israel treated it all so lightly—she thought nothing of committing adultery by worshiping idols made of wood and stone. So now the land has been polluted. But despite all this, her faithless sister Judah has never sincerely returned to me. She has only pretended to be sorry. I, the LORD, have spoken!" [Jeremiah 3:6-10]  **Figure 40: Prophet Jeremiah predicts that the Israelites will return from Babylonian exile.**
609 B.C.	**Jeremiah:** This is what the LORD of Heaven's Armies, the God of Israel, says: "When I bring them back from captivity, the people of Judah and its towns will again say, 'The LORD bless you, O righteous home, O holy mountain!'" [Jeremiah 31:23]

Timeline	Messages to the outcast
	The people of Judah regret their disobedience. Prophets encourage the people to re-establish their faith, because the punishment will end and the Jews will return to their homeland.
592 B.C.	**Ezekiel:** "So now, this is what the Sovereign LORD says: I will end the captivity of my people; I will have mercy on all Israel, for I jealously guard my holy reputation! They will accept responsibility for their past shame and unfaithfulness after they come home to live in peace in their own land, with no one to bother them. When I bring them home from the lands of their enemies, I will display my holiness among them for all the nations to see. Then my people will know that I am the LORD their God, because I sent them away to exile and brought them home again. I will leave none of my people behind. And I will never again turn my face from them, for I will pour out my Spirit upon the people of Israel. I, the Sovereign LORD, have spoken!" [Ezekiel 39:25-29]

Figure 41: Prophet Ezekiel encourages Jews during Babylonian exile.

Timeline	Messages to the humble
	The people of Judah return to Jerusalem poor and humiliated from their exile in Babylon. Prophets remind the Jews that God still loves them and He will strengthen the Jews as they rebuild their nation.
520 B.C.	**Haggai:** For this is what the LORD of Heaven's Armies says: In just a little while I will again shake the heavens and the earth, the oceans and the dry land. I will shake all the nations, and the treasures of all the nations will be brought to this Temple. I will fill this place with glory, says the LORD of Heaven's Armies. [Haggai 2:6-7]
520 B.C.	**Zechariah:** "I will strengthen Judah and save Israel; I will restore them because of my compassion. It will be as though I had never rejected them, for I am the LORD their God, who will hear their cries." [Zechariah 10:6]
458 B.C.	**Ezra:** But now we have been given a brief moment of grace, for the LORD our God has allowed a few of us to survive as a remnant. He has given us security in this holy place. Our God has brightened our eyes and granted us some relief from our slavery. For we were slaves, but in his unfailing love our God did not abandon us in our slavery. Instead, he caused the kings of Persia to treat us favorably. He revived us so we could rebuild the Temple of our God and repair its ruins. He has given us a protective wall in Judah and Jerusalem. [Ezra 9:8-9]

Figure 42: Prophet Ezra prays for the Jews.

Timeline	Messages to everyone
	Prophets confirm the Messiah's arrival, proclaim that the Savior is for all mankind, and announce that Jesus will return again in the future.
433 B.C.	**Malachi:** "Look! I am sending my messenger, and he will prepare the way before me. Then the Lord you are seeking will suddenly come to his Temple. The messenger of the covenant, whom you look for so eagerly, is surely coming," says the LORD of Heaven's Armies. [Malachi 3:1]
26 A.D.	**John the Baptist:** "Repent of your sins and turn to God, for the Kingdom of Heaven is near." [Matthew 3:2]
95 A.D.	**John the Beloved:** He who is the faithful witness to all these things says, "Yes, I am coming soon!" Amen! Come, Lord Jesus! May the grace of the Lord Jesus be with God's holy people. [Revelation 22:20]

Figure 43: Two Disciples walk to Emmaus with resurrected Jesus.

LAWS OF GOD

The Heart of God's Laws

Every culture in every age is founded on family, friendship, and government. All civilizations enact restrictions on their population as well as consequences for misbehavior. Although punishments may vary, laws around the globe are eerily similar. For instance, no civilization allows a citizen to kill another indiscriminately, or allows any type of sexual conduct at will. This similarity reveals the origins of moral conduct in our Creator, rather than in the differing populations. God provides all mankind with the moral compass, encapsulated in Ten Commandments provided to the Israelites and clarified by Jesus during His ministry.

- Jesus replied, "'You must love the LORD your God with all your heart, all your soul, and all your mind.' This is the first and greatest commandment. A second is equally important: 'Love your neighbor as yourself.' The entire law and all the demands of the prophets are based on these two commandments." [Matthew 22:37-40]
- Even Gentiles, who do not have God's written law, show that they know his law when they instinctively obey it, even without having heard it. [Romans 2:14]
- Oh, how I love your instructions! I think about them all day long. Your commands make me wiser than my enemies, for they are my constant guide. [Psalm 119:97-98]
- By his divine power, God has given us everything we need for living a godly life. We have received all of this by coming to know him, the one who called us to himself by means of his marvelous glory and excellence. And because of his glory and excellence, he has given us great and precious promises. These are the promises that enable you to share his divine nature and escape the world's corruption caused by human desires. [2 Peter 1:3-4]
- Until I get there, focus on reading the Scriptures to the church, encouraging the believers, and teaching them. [1 Timothy 4:13-16]
- When the LORD finished speaking with Moses on Mount Sinai, he gave him the two stone tablets inscribed with the terms of the covenant, written by the finger of God. [Exodus 31:18]

The First Commandment

"I am the LORD your God, who rescued you from the land of Egypt, the place of your slavery. You must not have any other god but me." [Exodus 20:2-3]

Humans are born entirely self-centered, requiring 24 x 7 care. Babies are at the mercy of their immediate and personal needs and desires, in other words, enslaved by thoughts of self. Maturity is largely based on progression from self-centered to God-centered selves, where thoughts of God and His Creation, including other people, outweigh personal gratification. The First Commandment depicts freedom from Israelite slavery in Egypt, but extends to each person's freedom from their self-centered nature.

- o But there is another power within me that is at war with my mind. This power makes me a slave to the sin that is still within me. Oh, what a miserable person I am! Who will free me from this life that is dominated by sin and death? Thank God! The answer is in Jesus Christ our Lord. So you see how it is: In my mind I really want to obey God's law, but because of my sinful nature I am a slave to sin. [Romans 7:23-25]
- o Gently instruct those who oppose the truth. Perhaps God will change those people's hearts, and they will learn the truth. Then they will come to their senses and escape from the devil's trap. For they have been held captive by him to do whatever he wants. [2 Timothy 2:25-26]
- o "No one can serve two masters. For you will hate one and love the other; you will be devoted to one and despise the other. You cannot serve both God and money." [Matthew 6:24]

The Second Commandment

"You must not make for yourself an idol of any kind or an image of anything in the heavens or on the earth or in the sea. You must not bow down to them or worship them, for I, the LORD your God, am a jealous God who will not tolerate your affection for any other gods. I lay the sins of the parents upon their children; the entire family is affected—even children in the third and fourth generations of those who reject me. But I lavish unfailing love for a thousand generations on those who love me and obey my commands." [Exodus 20:4-6]

Due to the connection with a Higher Authority, humans have an innate need to worship. If God-centered, then humans worship God. If not God-centered, humans find some alternative entity to worship, called idols in the Bible. The Second Commandment warns against worshipping idols.

- o The gods of other nations are mere idols, but the LORD made the heavens! [1 Chronicles 16:26]
- o "Do not tremble; do not be afraid. Did I not proclaim my purposes for you long ago? You are my witnesses—is there any other God? No! There is no other Rock—not one!" How foolish are those who manufacture idols. These prized objects are really worthless. The people who worship idols don't know this, so they are all put to shame. Who but a fool would make his own god—an idol that cannot help him one bit? All who worship idols will be disgraced along with all these craftsmen—mere humans—who claim they can make a god. They may all stand together, but they will stand in terror and shame. [Isaiah 44:8]

The Third Commandment

"You must not misuse the name of the LORD your God. The LORD will not let you go unpunished if you misuse his name." [Exodus 20:7]

Since worshipping God is not about what you do and don't do, it follows that the act of worship does not replace the relationship of God with His people. The Third Commandment warns people not to use the words, actions, and power of worship for anything except enhancing the relationship with God.

- "You must not misuse the name of the LORD your God. The LORD will not let you go unpunished if you misuse his name." [Exodus 20:7]
- And so the Lord says, "These people say they are mine. They honor me with their lips, but their hearts are far from me. And their worship of me is nothing but man-made rules learned by rote." [Isaiah 29:13]
- "What is this?" asks the LORD. "Why are my people enslaved again? Those who rule them shout in exultation. My name is blasphemed all day long." [Isaiah 52:5]
- Aren't they the ones who slander Jesus Christ, whose noble name you bear? [James 2:7]
- Avoid worthless, foolish talk that only leads to more godless behavior. [2 Timothy 2:16]

The Fourth Commandment

"Remember to observe the Sabbath day by keeping it holy. You have six days each week for your ordinary work, but the seventh day is a Sabbath day of rest dedicated to the LORD your God. On that day no one in your household may do any work. This includes you, your sons and daughters, your male and female servants, your livestock, and any foreigners living among you. For in six days the LORD made the heavens, the earth, the sea, and everything in them; but on the seventh day he rested. That is why the LORD blessed the Sabbath day and set it apart as holy." [Exodus 20:8-11]

Although the need to worship is innate in humans, the act of worship requires effort.

God tells people in the Fourth Commandment to set aside time to further their relationship with God.

Figure 44: The Disciples of Jesus pluck corn on the Sabbath, which is against the law of the Jewish leaders, but not against God's law concerning the Sabbath.

o "Keep the Sabbath day holy. Don't pursue your own interests on that day, but enjoy the Sabbath and speak of it with delight as the LORD's holy day. Honor the Sabbath in everything you do on that day, and don't follow your own desires or talk idly. Then the LORD will be your delight. I will give you great honor and satisfy you with the inheritance I promised to your ancestor Jacob. I, the LORD, have spoken!" [Isaiah 58:13-14]

o Jesus and his companions went to the town of Capernaum. When the Sabbath day came, he went into the synagogue and began to teach. [Mark 1:21]

o Jesus went into the synagogue again and noticed a man with a deformed hand. Since it was the Sabbath, Jesus' enemies watched him closely. If he healed the man's hand, they planned to accuse him of working on the Sabbath. Jesus said to the man with the deformed hand, "Come and stand in front of everyone." Then he turned to his critics and asked, "Does the law permit good deeds on the Sabbath, or is it a day for doing evil? Is this a day to save life or to destroy it?" But they wouldn't answer him. He looked around at them angrily and was deeply saddened by their hard hearts. Then he said to the man, "Hold out your hand." So the man held out his hand, and it was restored! [Mark 3:1-5]

The Fifth Commandment

"Honor your father and mother. Then you will live a long, full life in the land the LORD your God is giving you." [Exodus 20:12]

Biblical punishment for breaking the commandments is severe; death in the case of the Fifth Commandment for dishonoring one's parents. Although the punishment was literal in Old Testament times, the punishment still exists in the spiritual sense today. Something unseen dies when the parent/child relationship is broken. Studies show high rates of incarceration, suicide, behavioral disorders, and aggression among children of fatherless homes. In the New Testament, Jesus further demonstrates that one's practice of the Fifth Commandment is intricately linked with honoring God the Father.

o "Anyone who dishonors father or mother must be put to death. Such a person is guilty of a capital offense." [Leviticus 20:9]

Figure 45: Naomi and her Moabite daughter-in-law, Ruth, travel to Naomi's homeland, demonstrating an ideal parent/child relationship.

- For instance, God says, 'Honor your father and mother,' and 'Anyone who speaks disrespectfully of father or mother must be put to death.' But you say it is all right for people to say to their parents, 'Sorry, I can't help you. For I have vowed to give to God what I would have given to you.' In this way, you say they don't need to honor their parents. And so you cancel the word of God for the sake of your own tradition. [Matthew 15:4-6]
- "Yes," Jesus replied, "and I assure you that everyone who has given up house or brothers or sisters or mother or father or children or property, for my sake and for the Good News, will receive now in return a hundred times as many houses, brothers, sisters, mothers, children, and property—along with persecution. And in the world to come that person will have eternal life." [Mark 10:29-30]
- Standing near the cross were Jesus' mother, and his mother's sister, Mary (the wife of Clopas), and Mary Magdalene. When Jesus saw his mother standing there beside the disciple he loved, he said to her, "Dear woman, here is your son." And he said to this disciple, "Here is your mother." And from then on this disciple took her into his home. [John 19:25-27]

The Sixth Commandment
"You must not murder." [Exodus 20:13]

In the Sixth Commandment God explains that individuals do not have the authority to determine who should die. As a matter of fact, in the New Testament, Jesus further explains that the destructive emotion of rage in itself, whether or not it spurs action, is intolerable. By contrast, however, God does have the right to take or spare the life of an individual, since God the Creator can bring him or her back to life; or place him or her into an appropriate afterlife. By proxy, God's appointed governments have the authority to administer or withhold death as a means of punishment.

Figure 46: Jesus teaches in the synagogue. Jesus explains that disobedience includes dwelling on thoughts of rage as well as acts of rage.

- "These cities are for the protection of Israelites, foreigners living among you, and traveling merchants. Anyone who accidentally kills someone may flee there for safety. But if someone strikes and kills another person with a piece of iron, it is murder, and the murderer must be executed. Or if someone with a stone in his hand strikes and kills another person, it is murder, and the murderer must be put to death. [Numbers 35:15-17]

- o Anyone who hates another brother or sister is really a murderer at heart. And you know that murderers don't have eternal life within them. [1 John 3:15]
- o One of the prisoners at that time was Barabbas, a revolutionary who had committed murder in an uprising. The crowd went to Pilate and asked him to release a prisoner as usual. "Would you like me to release to you this 'King of the Jews'?" Pilate asked. (For he realized by now that the leading priests had arrested Jesus out of envy.) But at this point the leading priests stirred up the crowd to demand the release of Barabbas instead of Jesus. Pilate asked them, "Then what should I do with this man you call the king of the Jews?" They shouted back, "Crucify him!" [Mark 15:7-13]

The Seventh Commandment

"You must not commit adultery." [Exodus 20:14]

The Seventh Commandment explains that since God created family, only God has enough information to identify the members of each family. People who attempt to meet their personal needs outside of God's defined family damage their relationship with God.

- o "If a man commits adultery with his neighbor's wife, both the man and the woman who have committed adultery must be put to death." [Leviticus 20:10]
- o But the man who commits adultery is an utter fool, for he destroys himself. [Proverbs 6:32]
- o But I say, anyone who even looks at a woman with lust has already committed adultery with her in his heart. [Matthew 5:28]

Figure 47: Jesus forgives a woman caught in the act of adultery, even though adultery is a sin.

- o "Teacher," they said to Jesus, "this woman was caught in the act of adultery. The law of Moses says to stone her. What do you say?" They were trying to trap him into saying something they could use against him, but Jesus stooped down and wrote in the dust with his finger. They kept demanding an answer, so he stood up again and said, "All right, but let the one who has never sinned throw the first stone!" Then he stooped down again and wrote in the dust. When the accusers heard this, they slipped away one by one, beginning with the oldest, until only Jesus was left in the middle of the crowd with the woman. Then Jesus stood up again and said to the woman, "Where are your accusers? Didn't even one of them condemn you?" "No, Lord," she said. And Jesus said, "Neither do I. Go and sin no more." [John 8:4-11]

"You must not steal." [Exodus 20:15]

God demonstrates love by giving, as in John 3:16, "For God loved the world so much that he gave his one and only Son, so that everyone who believes in him will not perish but have eternal life." Taking, or stealing, is the opposite of giving, so the ability to give reveals whether or not a person is God-centered.

Figure 48: Using a whip, Jesus drives corrupt, greedy merchants out of the temple.

- "Should people cheat God? Yet you have cheated me! But you ask, 'What do you mean? When did we ever cheat you?' You have cheated me of the tithes and offerings due to me. You are under a curse, for your whole nation has been cheating me. Bring all the tithes into the storehouse so there will be enough food in my Temple. If you do," says the LORD of Heaven's Armies, "I will open the windows of heaven for you. I will pour out a blessing so great you won't have enough room to take it in! Try it! Put me to the test!" [Malachi 3:8-10]
- Jesus entered the Temple and began to drive out all the people buying and selling animals for sacrifice. He knocked over the tables of the money changers and the chairs of those selling doves. He said to them, "The Scriptures declare, 'My Temple will be called a house of prayer,' but you have turned it into a den of thieves!" [Matthew 21:12-13]
- If you are a thief, quit stealing. Instead, use your hands for good hard work, and then give generously to others in need. [Ephesians 4:28]
- And all the believers met together in one place and shared everything they had. They sold their property and possessions and shared the money with those in need. [Acts 2:44-45]

The Ninth Commandment

"You must not testify falsely against your neighbor." [Exodus 20:16]

The ability to tell the truth reveals the object of our worship, whether God, devil or an idol.

Figure 49: Disciple Simon Peter lies by denying his identity as one of Jesus' disciples.

- o The LORD God placed the man in the Garden of Eden to tend and watch over it. But the LORD God warned him, "You may freely eat the fruit of every tree in the garden—except the tree of the knowledge of good and evil. If you eat its fruit, you are sure to die." [Genesis 2:15-17]
- o "You won't die!" the serpent replied to the woman. "God knows that your eyes will be opened as soon as you eat it, and you will be like God, knowing both good and evil." [Genesis 3:4-5]
- o He was a murderer from the beginning. He has always hated the truth, because there is no truth in him. When he lies, it is consistent with his character; for he is a liar and the father of lies. [John 8:44]
- o Meanwhile, Peter was in the courtyard below. One of the servant girls who worked for the high priest came by and noticed Peter warming himself at the fire. She looked at him closely and said, "You were one of those with Jesus of Nazareth." But Peter denied it. "I don't know what you're talking about," he said, and he went out into the entryway. Just then, a rooster crowed. When the servant girl saw him standing there, she began telling the others, "This man is definitely one of them!" But Peter denied it again. A little later some of the other bystanders confronted Peter and said, "You must be one of them, because you are a Galilean." Peter swore, "A curse on me if I'm lying—I don't know this man you're talking about!" And immediately the rooster crowed the second time. Suddenly, Jesus' words flashed through Peter's mind: "Before the rooster crows twice, you will deny three times that you even know me." And he broke down and wept. [Mark 14:66-72]
- o We reject all shameful deeds and underhanded methods. We don't try to trick anyone or distort the word of God. We tell the truth before God, and all who are honest know this. [2 Corinthians 4:2]

The Tenth Commandment

"You must not covet your neighbor's house. You must not covet your neighbor's wife, male or female servant, ox or donkey, or anything else that belongs to your neighbor." [Exodus 20:17]

Commandments five through nine clarify that a damaging emotion, whether or not it results in action, is enough to interfere with one's relationship with God. The Tenth Commandment identifies that damaging emotion: a longing for something that someone else has, or coveting. God-centered people strive to desire only what God wants for them.

- Yet true godliness with contentment is itself great wealth. After all, we brought nothing with us when we came into the world, and we can't take anything with us when we leave it. So if we have enough food and clothing, let us be content. But people who long to be rich fall into temptation and are trapped by many foolish and harmful desires that plunge them into ruin and destruction. For the love of money is the root of all kinds of evil. And some people, craving money, have wandered from the true faith and pierced themselves with many sorrows. [1 Timothy 6:6-10]
- What is causing the quarrels and fights among you? Don't they come from the evil desires at war within you? You want what you don't have, so you scheme and kill to get it. You are jealous of what others have, but you can't get it, so you fight and wage war to take it away from them. Yet you don't have what you want because you don't ask God for it. And even when you ask, you don't get it because your motives are all wrong—you want only what will give you pleasure. [James 4:1-3]
- Then someone called from the crowd, "Teacher, please tell my brother to divide our father's estate with me." Jesus replied, "Friend, who made me a judge over you to decide such things as that?" Then he said, "Beware! Guard against every kind of greed. Life is not measured by how much you own." [Luke 12:13-15]

The Greatest Commandment

In the New Testament, Jesus sums up the Ten Commandments by echoing words written in the Old Testament, loosely translated as "Love God" and "Love Others."

- "Do not seek revenge or bear a grudge against a fellow Israelite, but love your neighbor as yourself. I am the LORD. You must obey all my decrees." [Leviticus 19:18 -19]
- And you must love the LORD your God with all your heart, all your soul, and all your strength. And you must commit yourselves wholeheartedly to these commands that I am giving you today. [Deuteronomy 6:5-6]
- Jesus replied, "'You must love the LORD your God with all your heart, all your soul, and all your mind.' This is the first and greatest commandment. A second is equally important: 'Love your neighbor as yourself.' The entire law and all the demands of the prophets are based on these two commandments." [Matthew 22:37-40]
- For the commandments say, "You must not commit adultery. You must not murder. You must not steal. You must not covet." These—and other such commandments—are summed up in this one commandment: "Love your neighbor as yourself." Love does no wrong to others, so love fulfills the requirements of God's law. [Romans 13:9-10]

For the word of God is alive and powerful. It is sharper than the sharpest two-edged sword, cutting between soul and spirit, between joint and marrow. It exposes our innermost thoughts and desires.   --Hebrews 4:12

HEAVEN AND THE ANGELS

Study of Heaven

Misunderstandings concerning Heaven and Angels are common because many people want the protection of the Angels and the hope of Heaven without the burden of God's laws. This chapter, Heaven and the Angels, contains Bible verses in order to clarify the contrast between Heaven and Earth as well as Angels and People. Heaven is the home of Angels and Believers while Earth is the temporary home of People. Although the Bible doesn't shy away from speaking of hell, there is more emphasis placed on descriptions of heaven.

Heaven and Earth have some things in common.

God creates both Heaven and Earth.
- o In the beginning God created the heavens and the earth. [Genesis 1:1]

God fills all Heaven and Earth:
- o "Can anyone hide from me in a secret place? Am I not everywhere in all the heavens and earth?" says the LORD. [Jeremiah 23:24]

Both Earth and Heaven have an entrance and an exit.
- o He opened the heavens and came down; dark storm clouds were beneath his feet. [Psalm 18:9]
- o Then I saw heaven opened, and a white horse was standing there. Its rider was named Faithful and True, for he judges fairly and wages a righteous war. [Revelation 19:11]

God corrects beings in both Heaven and Earth.
- o In that day the LORD will punish the gods in the heavens and the proud rulers of the nations on earth. [Isaiah 24:21]

Both Heaven and Earth have laws.
- o Do you know the laws of the universe? Can you use them to regulate the earth? [Job 38:33]
- o But this is what the LORD says: I would no more reject my people than I would change my laws that govern night and day, earth and sky. [Jeremiah 33:25]

Believers are citizens in both Heaven and Earth.
- o But we are citizens of heaven, where the Lord Jesus Christ lives. And we are eagerly waiting for him to return as our Savior. [Philippians 3:20]
- o For he raised us from the dead along with Christ and seated us with him in the heavenly realms because we are united with Christ Jesus. [Ephesians 2:6]

Heaven and Earth are also very different.

God's will is done in Heaven, but not consistently on Earth.
- o   May your Kingdom come soon. May your will be done on earth, as it is in heaven. [Matthew 6:10]

God's throne and sanctuary are in Heaven, not on Earth.
- o   **The LORD has made the heavens his throne; from there he rules over everything. [Psalm 103:19]**
- o   **This is what the LORD says: "Heaven is my throne, and the earth is my footstool. Could you build me a temple as good as that? Could you build me such a resting place?" [Isaiah 66:1]**

Figure 50: An angel assists Jesus as He agonizes in the Garden of Gethsemane.

Not all people will end up in Heaven.
- o   **"Not everyone who calls out to me, 'Lord! Lord!' will enter the Kingdom of Heaven. Only those who actually do the will of my Father in heaven will enter." [Matthew 7:21]**
- o   **"Everyone who acknowledges me publicly here on earth, I will also acknowledge before my Father in heaven." [Matthew 10:32]**

God's blessings originate in Heaven, not Earth.
- o   **"Bring all the tithes into the storehouse so there will be enough food in my Temple. If you do," says the LORD of Heaven's Armies, "I will open the windows of heaven for you. I will pour out a blessing so great you won't have enough room to take it in! Try it! Put me to the test!" [Malachi 3:10]**

Heaven is bustling with activity. Believers serve God while in Heaven.

- o No longer will there be a curse upon anything. For the throne of God and of the Lamb will be there, and his servants will worship him. [Revelation 22:3]

Satan worked in Heaven until God expelled him from Heaven to Earth.

- o Your rich commerce led you to violence, and you sinned.
  So I banished you in disgrace from the mountain of God. [Ezekiel 28:16]

Believers learn while in Heaven.

- o Now we see things imperfectly, like puzzling reflections in a mirror, but then we will see everything with perfect clarity. All that I know now is partial and incomplete, but then I will know everything completely, just as God now knows me completely. [1 Corinthians 13:12]

Figure 51: Three disciples observe a glorified Jesus speaking with Prophet Moses and Prophet Elijah.

Believers reign with God while in Heaven.

- o If we endure hardship, we will reign with him. If we deny him, he will deny us. [2 Timothy 2:12]

Believers worship God while in Heaven.

- o Whenever the living beings give glory and honor and thanks to the one sitting on the throne (the one who lives forever and ever), the twenty-four elders fall down and worship the one sitting on the throne (the one who lives forever and ever). And they lay their crowns before the throne and say, "You are worthy, O Lord our God, to receive glory and honor and power. For you created all things, and they exist because you created what you pleased." [Revelation 4:9-11]

Believers judge other beings while in Heaven.

- o Don't you realize that someday we believers will judge the world? And since you are going to judge the world, can't you decide even these little things among yourselves? Don't you realize that we will judge angels? So you should surely be able to resolve ordinary disputes in this life. [1 Corinthians 6:2-3]

Earth is not Heaven!

Believers will suffer here on Earth no matter how close a walk they have with Christ.

- o For you have been given not only the privilege of trusting in Christ but also the privilege of suffering for him. We are in this struggle together. You have seen my struggle in the past, and you know that I am still in the midst of it. [Philippians 1:29]
- o For God called you to do good, even if it means suffering, just as Christ suffered for you. He is your example, and you must follow in his steps. [1 Peter 2:21]

Although suffering prepares people for glory, Believers are not to seek it out, but to live their lives as blessings to all in this world.

- o "God blesses those who are persecuted for doing right, for the Kingdom of Heaven is theirs. God blesses you when people mock you and persecute you and lie about you and say all sorts of evil things

Figure 52: Unbelievers mock Jesus. Jesus warns Believers to expect similar behavior.

against you because you are my followers. Be happy about it! Be very glad! For a great reward awaits you in heaven. And remember, the ancient prophets were persecuted in the same way. You are the salt of the earth. But what good is salt if it has lost its flavor? Can you make it salty again? It will be thrown out and trampled underfoot as worthless. You are the light of the world—like a city on a hilltop that cannot be hidden. No one lights a lamp and then puts it under a basket. Instead, a lamp is placed on a stand, where it gives light to everyone in the house. In the same way, let your good deeds shine out for all to see, so that everyone will praise your heavenly Father." [Matthew 5:10-16]

Believers do not become angels upon arrival in Heaven.

A Believer's human identity is already in heaven and remains that way.

- o For he raised us from the dead along with Christ and seated us with him in the heavenly realms because we are united with Christ Jesus. [Ephesians 2:6]

Jesus is not an angel.

Although Jesus is referred to as "The Angel of the Lord" in the Old Testament, Jesus is fully man and fully God, but not an angelic being. Some Angels in the Old Testament are referred to as "An Angel of the Lord." Notice the difference in the definitive article "the" versus the indefinite article "an" when referring to Jesus as "The Angel of the Lord."

- o This shows that the Son is far greater than the angels, just as the name God gave him is greater than their names. [Hebrews 1:4]

Humans and Angels have many things in common.

Both angels and humans are created beings.
- o Christ is the visible image of the invisible God. He existed before anything was created and is supreme over all creation, for through him God created everything in the heavenly realms and on earth. He made the things we can see and the things we can't see—such as thrones, kingdoms, rulers, and authorities in the unseen world. Everything was created through him and for him. [Colossians 1:15-16]

Both angels and humans have voices.
- o And then I heard every creature in heaven and on earth and under the earth and in the sea. They sang: "Blessing and honor and glory and power belong to the one sitting on the throne and to the Lamb forever and ever." [Revelation 5:13]

Both angels and humans have language.
- o If I could speak all the languages of earth and of angels, but didn't love others, I would only be a noisy gong or a clanging cymbal. [1 Corinthians 13:1]

Both angels and humans are intuitive.
- o Then the angel spoke to the women. "Don't be afraid!" he said. "I know you are looking for Jesus, who was crucified." [Matthew 28:5]

Both angels and humans have emotions.
- o What supports its foundations, and who laid its cornerstone as the morning stars sang together and all the angels shouted for joy? [Job 38:6-7]

Both angels and humans have will.
- o And I remind you of the angels who did not stay within the limits of authority God gave them but left the place where they belonged. God has kept them securely chained in prisons of darkness, waiting for the great day of judgment. [Jude 1:6]

Both angels and humans have knowledge, although the knowledge differs, since angels know whom God has chosen and humans don't.
- o And he will send out his angels with the mighty blast of a trumpet, and they will gather his chosen ones from all over the world—from the farthest ends of the earth and heaven. [Matthew 24:31]

Both angels and humans have power.
- o So you see, the Lord knows how to rescue godly people from their trials, even while keeping the wicked under punishment until the day of final judgment. He is especially hard on those who follow their own twisted sexual desire, and who despise authority. These people are proud and arrogant, daring even to scoff at supernatural beings without so much as trembling. But the angels, who are far greater in power and strength, do not dare to bring from the Lord a charge of blasphemy against those supernatural beings. [2 Peter 2:9-11]

Humans and Angels have many things in common.

Both angels and humans have hierarchy. Angels have different levels of authority, including archangels in charge of warrior angels; seraphim that attend to God's throne; and cherubim that guard access.

- But for twenty-one days the spirit prince of the kingdom of Persia blocked my way. Then Michael, one of the archangels, came to help me, and I left him there with the spirit prince of the kingdom of Persia. [Daniel 10:13]

- It was in the year King Uzziah died that I saw the Lord. He was sitting on a lofty throne, and the train of his robe filled the Temple. Attending him were mighty seraphim, each having six wings. With two wings they covered their faces, with two they covered their feet, and with two they flew. They were calling out to each other, "Holy, holy, holy is the LORD of Heaven's Armies! The whole earth is filled with his glory!" [Isaiah 6:1-3]

Figure 53: Three angels bring a message to Patriarch Abraham.

- Then the LORD God said, "Look, the human beings have become like us, knowing both good and evil. What if they reach out, take fruit from the tree of life, and eat it? Then they will live forever!" So the LORD God banished them from the Garden of Eden, and he sent Adam out to cultivate the ground from which he had been made. After sending them out, the LORD God stationed mighty cherubim to the east of the Garden of Eden. And he placed a flaming sword that flashed back and forth to guard the way to the tree of life. [Genesis 3:22-24]

Angels and humans can only be in one place at one time.

- As I was praying, Gabriel, whom I had seen in the earlier vision, came swiftly to me at the time of the evening sacrifice. He explained to me, "Daniel, I have come here to give you insight and understanding. The moment you began praying, a command was given. And now I am here to tell you what it was, for you are very precious to God. Listen carefully so that you can understand the meaning of your vision." [Daniel 9:21-23]

Angels and humans worship God.

- Each of these living beings had six wings, and their wings were covered all over with eyes, inside and out. Day after day and night after night they keep on saying, "Holy, holy, holy is the Lord God, the Almighty—the one who always was, who is, and who is still to come." [Revelation 4:8]

Humans and Angels are also very different.

Although angels can take on human form, angels do not have human bodies.
- o Don't forget to show hospitality to strangers, for some who have done this have entertained angels without realizing it! [Hebrews 13:2]

Humans have dominion over the earth.
- o Then God said, "Let us make human beings in our image, to be like us. They will reign over the fish in the sea, the birds in the sky, the livestock, all the wild animals on the earth, and the small animals that scurry along the ground." [Genesis 1:26]

Humans have families, but angels do not marry or reproduce.
- o For when the dead rise, they will neither marry nor be given in marriage. In this respect they will be like the angels in heaven. [Matthew 22:30]
- o For when the dead rise, they will neither marry nor be given in marriage. In this respect they will be like the angels in heaven. [Mark 12:25]

Human Believers, but not angels, must be adopted to be children of God.
- o God decided in advance to adopt us into his own family by bringing us to himself through Jesus Christ. This is what he wanted to do, and it gave him great pleasure. [Ephesians 1:5]

Figure 54: An angel appears to Leader Joshua and the Israelites.

Angels do not die. Once in Heaven, people do not die either.
- o And they will never die again. In this respect they will be like angels. They are children of God and children of the resurrection. [Luke 20:36]

Angels are Busy

Angels worship God.

- o   Each of these living beings had six wings, and their wings were covered all over with eyes, inside and out. Day after day and night after night they keep on saying, "Holy, holy, holy is the Lord God, the Almighty—the one who always was, who is, and who is still to come." [Revelation 4:8]

Angels minister to Christ.

- o   "Get out of here, Satan," Jesus told him. "For the Scriptures say, 'You must worship the LORD your God and serve only him.'" Then the devil went away, and angels came and took care of Jesus. [Matthew 4:10-11]

Angels carry out God's will.

- o   Praise the LORD, you angels, you mighty ones who carry out his plans, listening for each of his commands. [Psalm 103:20]

Figure 55: An angel assists Prophet Elijah.

Angels protect God's people.

- o   For he will order his angels to protect you wherever you go. [Psalm 91:11]

Angels assist Believers at death.

- o   "Finally, the poor man died and was carried by the angels to be with Abraham. The rich man also died and was buried, and his soul went to the place of the dead. There, in torment, he saw Abraham in the far distance with Lazarus at his side." [Luke 16:22-23]

Even though angels are in the presence of the Lord, they serve Believers on earth.

- o   Therefore, angels are only servants—spirits sent to care for people who will inherit salvation. [Hebrews 1:14]

Satan was an angel who sinned in the heavenly workplace.

- o You defiled your sanctuaries with your many sins and your dishonest trade. [Ezekiel 28:18]

One-third of the angels decide against being of service to God and man, and choose to follow Satan.

- o His tail swept away one-third of the stars in the sky, and he threw them to the earth. [Revelation 12:4a]

The one-third of the angels that followed Satan are called fallen angels or demons. They have no hope of salvation.

- o And the dragon lost the battle, and he and his angels were forced out of heaven. This great dragon—the ancient serpent called the devil, or Satan, the one deceiving the whole world—was thrown down to the earth with all his angels. [Revelation 12:8-9]

Figure 56: An angel describes a vision of four chariots to Disciple John concerning prophecy still to come.

Although demons are intelligent and strong, they are morally wicked.

- o One day as we were going down to the place of prayer, we met a demon-possessed slave girl. She was a fortune-teller who earned a lot of money for her masters. [Acts 16:16]
- o This man lived among the burial caves and could no longer be restrained, even with a chain. [Mark 5:3]
- o For we are not fighting against flesh-and-blood enemies, but against evil rulers and authorities of the unseen world, against mighty powers in this dark world, and against evil spirits in the heavenly places. [Ephesians 6:12]

Humans will judge the fallen angels.

- o Don't you realize that we will judge angels? So you should surely be able to resolve ordinary disputes in this life. [1 Corinthians 6:3]

Putting on the spiritual armor of God protects Believers against Satan and his followers..

- o Put on all of God's armor so that you will be able to stand firm against all strategies of the devil. [Ephesians 6:11]

Angels and Humans

Jesus is crowned with glory and honor, and **Believers** share in Christ's exaltation, thus **Believers** share in his glory.

- o "I have given them the glory you gave me, so they may be one as we are one." [John 17:22]
- o So now Jesus and the ones he makes holy have the same Father. That is why Jesus is not ashamed to call them his brothers and sisters. [Hebrews 2:11]
- o We also know that the Son did not come to help angels; he came to help the descendants of Abraham. [Hebrews 2:16]

Angels and humans have ways to understand each other, but it's possible that people will ignore the message.

- o "See, I am sending an angel before you to protect you on your journey and lead you safely to the place I have prepared for you. Pay close attention to him, and obey his instructions. Do not rebel against him, for he is my representative, and he will not forgive your rebellion." [Exodus 23:20-21]

Figure 57: Patriarch Jacob wrestles with an angel before reuniting with his brother Esau.

Believers need to pay attention to hear angels.

- o Suddenly, an angel of the Lord appeared among them, and the radiance of the Lord's glory surrounded them. They were terrified, but the angel reassured them. "Don't be afraid!" he said. "I bring you good news that will bring great joy to all people. The Savior—yes, the Messiah, the Lord—has been born today in Bethlehem, the city of David!" [Luke 2:9-11]

GENESIS AND REVELATION

God is hard at work and finishes what He starts. This chapter, Genesis and Revelation, explores the contrast between what God starts in the first book of the Bible and how God completes the process in the last book of the Bible.

- o And I am certain that God, who began the good work within you, will continue his work until it is finally finished on the day when Christ Jesus returns. [Philippians 1:6]
- o But Jesus replied, "My Father is always working, and so am I." [John 5:17]

Creation

God is the Creator, and the current Heaven and Earth are not the finished product.

The creation of heaven and earth.

- o In the beginning God created the heavens and the earth. [Genesis 1:1]
- o So the creation of the heavens and the earth and everything in them was completed. [Genesis 2:1]

The creation of the new heaven and earth.

- o Then I saw a new heaven and a new earth, for the old heaven and the old earth had disappeared. And the sea was also gone. [Revelation 21:1]

Mankind was meant to live and dwell with God.

When Adam and Eve are expelled from the Garden of Eden, mankind no longer walks directly with God. However, that will be remedied.

Mankind is meant to live with God forever.

- o When the cool evening breezes were blowing, the man and his wife heard the LORD God walking about in the garden. [Genesis 3:8]
- o "Of course we may eat fruit from the trees in the garden," the woman replied. "It's only the fruit from the tree in the middle of the garden that we are not allowed to eat. God said, 'You must not eat it or even touch it; if you do, you will die.'" [Genesis 3:2-3]

God lives with mankind again after the End of the Age.

- o I heard a loud shout from the throne, saying, "Look, God's home is now among his people! He will live with them, and they will be his people. God himself will be with them." [Revelation 21:3]
- o And they will see his face, and his name will be written on their foreheads. And there will be no night there—no need for lamps or sun—for the Lord God will shine on them. And they will reign forever and ever. [Revelation 22:4-5]

Safe Haven for mankind

The Garden of Eden is a safe haven for Adam and Eve. Earth is not a safe haven currently, but God will remedy that at the End of the Age.

Sanctuary in the Garden of Eden, including the river and the Tree of Life.
- o Then the LORD God planted a garden in Eden in the east, and there he placed the man he had made. The LORD God made all sorts of trees grow up from the ground—trees that were beautiful and that produced delicious fruit. In the middle of the garden he placed the tree of life and the tree of the knowledge of good and evil. A river flowed from the land of Eden, watering the garden and then dividing into four branches. [Genesis 2:8-10]

Sanctuary in the New Jerusalem, the river and the Tree of Life.
- o So he took me in the Spirit to a great, high mountain, and he showed me the holy city, Jerusalem, descending out of heaven from God. It shone with the glory of God and sparkled like a precious stone—like jasper as clear as crystal. [Revelation 21:10-11]
- o Then the angel showed me a river with the water of life, clear as crystal, flowing from the throne of God and of the Lamb. It flowed down the center of the main street. On each side of the river grew a tree of life, bearing twelve crops of fruit, with a fresh crop each month. The leaves were used for medicine to heal the nations.
[Revelation 22:1-2]

God punishes mankind

God punishes, in the form of a curse, mankind for disobedience. The curse is eliminated at the End of the Age.

The curse is introduced.
- o Then he (God) said to the woman, "I will sharpen the pain of your pregnancy, and in pain you will give birth. And you will desire to control your husband, but he will rule over you." And to the man he said, "Since you listened to your wife and ate from the tree whose fruit I commanded you not to eat, the ground is cursed because of you. All your life you will struggle to scratch a living from it. It will grow thorns and thistles for you, though you will eat of its grains." [Genesis 3:16-18]

The curse is abolished at the End of the Age.
- o No longer will there be a curse upon anything. For the throne of God and of the Lamb will be there, and his servants will worship him. [Revelation 22:3]

Mankind succumbs to Satan's temptation, leading to a broken relationship with God. God remedies that by providing Believers protection from the enemy:

Mankind is vulnerable to evil.

- o "You won't die!" the serpent replied to the woman. "God knows that your eyes will be opened as soon as you eat it, and you will be like God, knowing both good and evil." The woman was convinced. She saw that the tree was beautiful and its fruit looked delicious, and she wanted the wisdom it would give her. So she took some of the fruit and ate it. Then she gave some to her husband, who was with her, and he ate it, too. [Genesis 3:4-6]

Figure 58: Prophecy still to come includes a vision from Disciple John of our future protection from Satan.

Believers are protected from evil now and in the future.

- o But the Lord is faithful; he will strengthen you and guard you from the evil one. [2 Thessalonians 3:3]
- o When the dragon realized that he had been thrown down to the earth, he pursued the woman who had given birth to the male child. But she was given two wings like those of a great eagle so she could fly to the place prepared for her in the wilderness. There she would be cared for and protected from the dragon for a time, times, and half a time. [Revelation 12:13-14]

Mankind experiences death.

God limits sin by providing restraints, even death, since individuals can no longer sin once they have died. Believers experience physical death; unbelievers experience a spiritual death as well.

Death enters creation.
- o "By the sweat of your brow will you have food to eat until you return to the ground from which you were made. For you were made from dust, and to dust you will return." [Genesis 3:19]

Death is destroyed.
- o Then death and the grave were thrown into the lake of fire. This lake of fire is the second death. And anyone whose name was not found recorded in the Book of Life was thrown into the lake of fire. [Revelation 20:14-15]

Figure 59: Disciple John has a vision of death.

God allows groups of unfaithful people for a time to give them a chance to follow Him, but at some point, God eliminates the unfaithful nations.

Babylon is built.

o   Cush was also the ancestor of Nimrod, who was the first heroic warrior on earth. Since he was the greatest hunter in the world, his name became proverbial. People would say, "This man is like Nimrod, the greatest hunter in the world." He built his kingdom in the land of Babylonia, with the cities of Babylon, Erech, Akkad, and Calneh. [Genesis 10:8-10]

o   I am raising up the Babylonians, a cruel and violent people. They will march across the world and conquer other lands. [Habakkuk 1:6]

Figure 60: Disciple John has a vision of Babylon fallen, symbolic for the destruction of the civilization of unbelievers.

Babylon is destroyed.

o   And I saw another angel flying through the sky, carrying the eternal Good News to proclaim to the people who belong to this world—to every nation, tribe, language, and people. "Fear God," he shouted. "Give glory to him. For the time has come when he will sit as judge. Worship him who made the heavens, the earth, the sea, and all the springs of water." Then another angel followed him through the sky, shouting, "Babylon is fallen—that great city is fallen—because she made all the nations of the world drink the wine of her passionate immorality." [Revelation 14:6-8]

God Brings His People back to Him at the End of Age

At the End of the Age, Satan is cast into the lake of fire with his followers, and Believers once again dwell with God.

Man is no longer banished from God
- So the LORD God banished them from the Garden of Eden…. [Genesis 3:23]
- I heard a loud shout from the throne, saying, "Look, God's home is now among his people! He will live with them, and they will be his people. God himself will be with them. [Revelation 21:3]

God accepts sacrifices as a price to be paid for the sinfulness of man.
- Then Abraham looked up and saw a ram caught by its horns in a thicket. So he took the ram and sacrificed it as a burnt offering in place of his son. [Genesis 22:13]
- For you were slaughtered, and your blood has ransomed people for God from every tribe and language and people and nation. [Revelation 5:9]

The evil work of the serpent Satan is eliminated forever.
- "The serpent deceived me," she replied. [Genesis 3:13]
- He seized the dragon—that old serpent, who is the devil, Satan—and bound him in chains for a thousand years. [Revelation 20:2]
- Then the devil, who had deceived them, was thrown into the fiery lake of burning sulfur, joining the beast and the false prophet. There they will be tormented day and night forever and ever. [Revelation 20:10]

God blesses Believers for all time.
- For Abraham will certainly become a great and mighty nation, and all the nations of the earth will be blessed through him. [Genesis 18:18]
- All who are victorious will inherit all these blessings, and I will be their God, and they will be my children. [Revelation 21:7]
- All who are victorious will become pillars in the Temple of my God, and they will never have to leave it. And I will write on them the name of my God, and they will be citizens in the city of my God—the new Jerusalem that comes down from heaven from my God. And I will also write on them my new name. [Revelation 3:12]

Figure 61: At the End of the Age, Believers live in New Jerusalem.

BLESSINGS

God has provided many blessings for individuals to form a closer relationship with Him.

Promises

God has good things in mind for us.

- o "For I know the plans I have for you," says the LORD. "They are plans for good and not for disaster, to give you a future and a hope." [Jeremiah 29:11]
- o What shall we say about such wonderful things as these? If God is for us, who can ever be against us? [Romans 8:31]
- o I press on to reach the end of the race and receive the heavenly prize for which God, through Christ Jesus, is calling us. [Philippians 3:14]

Work

The first assignment for Adam is tending the Garden of Eden as a gift, not a punishment. Work becomes punishing when Adam is exiled from the Garden of Eden and he has to struggle to accomplish his work. Through God, our work is once again rewarding.

- o The LORD God placed the man in the Garden of Eden to tend and watch over it. [Genesis 2:15]
- o "By the sweat of your brow will you have food to eat until you return to the ground from which you were made. For you were made from dust, and to dust you will return." [Genesis 3:19]
- o "Look, I am coming soon, bringing my reward with me to repay all people according to their deeds." [Revelation 22:12]

Figure 62: Adam struggles to provide food for his family when he sins against God.

Family

God's creation is completed upon commencement of the first family provided in the Garden of Eden. Adam is overjoyed, because family is a gift. Family relationships become painful through anger, selfishness, and divorce. In Heaven, individual families aren't necessary, because everyone is in the Family of God.

Figure 63: God blesses families that overcome difficulties to stay intact.

- o "At last!" the man exclaimed. "This one is bone from my bone, and flesh from my flesh! She will be called 'woman,' because she was taken from 'man.'" [Genesis 2:23]
- o Jesus replied, "Moses permitted divorce only as a concession to your hard hearts, but it was not what God had originally intended." [Matthew 19:8]
- o But those who won't care for their relatives, especially those in their own household, have denied the true faith. Such people are worse than unbelievers. [1 Timothy 5:8]
- o So now you Gentiles are no longer strangers and foreigners. You are citizens along with all of God's holy people. You are members of God's family. [Ephesians 2:19]

Wisdom

People are made in the image of God, so humans have a capacity for knowledge, which helps us to understand God's ways, and with humble obedience, results in being blessed with wisdom. Gaining wisdom becomes painful when someone wants to know as much as God or takes shortcuts to obtain knowledge or wisdom.

- o For the Lord grants wisdom! From his mouth come knowledge and understanding. [Proverbs 2:6]
- o The woman was convinced. She saw that the tree was beautiful and its fruit looked delicious, and she wanted the wisdom it would give her. So she took some of the fruit and ate it. Then she gave some to her husband, who was with her, and he ate it, too. [Genesis 3:6]
- o A mocker seeks wisdom and never finds it, but knowledge comes easily to those with understanding. [Proverbs 14:6]
- o Yet when I am among mature believers, I do speak with words of wisdom, but not the kind of wisdom that belongs to this world or to the rulers of this world, who are soon forgotten. No, the wisdom we speak of is the mystery of God—his plan that was previously hidden, even though he made it for our ultimate glory before the world began. But the rulers of this world have not understood it; if they had, they would not have crucified our glorious Lord. [1 Corinthians 2:6-8]

Human Beauty

People are made in the image of God, so humans are beautiful. Beauty becomes painful when a person prefers outer beauty to inner beauty. God implores people to focus on inner beauty, because that's what accompanies Believers to Heaven.

Figure 64: Rebekkah is chosen to be Patriarch Isaac's bride because of both her outer beauty and her generous spirit.

- o Thank you for making me so wonderfully complex! Your workmanship is marvelous—how well I know it. [Psalm 139:14]
- o But the LORD said to Samuel, "Don't judge by his appearance or height, for I have rejected him. The LORD doesn't see things the way you see them. People judge by outward appearance, but the LORD looks at the heart." [1 Samuel 16:7]
- o Don't be concerned about the outward beauty of fancy hairstyles, expensive jewelry, or beautiful clothes. You should clothe yourselves instead with the beauty that comes from within, the unfading beauty of a gentle and quiet spirit, which is so precious to God. [1 Peter 3:3-4]
- o "Physical training is good, but training for godliness is much better, promising benefits in this life and in the life to come." [1 Timothy 4:8]

Pain

Pain is universal. The purpose of pain is spiritual growth, which is a blessing. An individual is never alone in his or her pain. Believers do not take pain with them to Heaven.

- o Stand firm against him, and be strong in your faith. Remember that your Christian brothers and sisters all over the world are going through the same kind of suffering you are. [1 Peter 5:9]
- o Now I am glad I sent it, not because it hurt you, but because the pain caused you to repent and change your ways. It was the kind of sorrow God wants his people to have, so you were not harmed by us in any way. For the kind of sorrow God wants us to experience leads us away from sin and results in salvation. There's no regret for that kind of sorrow. But worldly sorrow, which lacks repentance, results in spiritual death. [2 Corinthians 7:9-10]
- o The LORD is close to the brokenhearted; he rescues those whose spirits are crushed. [Psalm 34:18]
- o "He will wipe every tear from their eyes, and there will be no more death or sorrow or crying or pain. All these things are gone forever." [Revelation 21:4]

Self

Adam and Eve became self-aware as a result of the Original Sin. Now, the blessing of spiritual growth consists of becoming more conscious of God and less aware of self. Although Believers retain individual identity, self fuels feelings of separateness and has no value in Heaven.

- o At that moment their eyes were opened, and they suddenly felt shame at their nakedness. So they sewed fig leaves together to cover themselves. [Genesis 3:7]
- o "He must become greater and greater, and I must become less and less." [John 3:30]
- o Then Jesus said to his disciples, "If any of you wants to be my follower, you must turn from your selfish ways, take up your cross, and follow me. If you try to hang on to your life, you will lose it. But if you give up your life for my sake, you will save it. [Matthew 16:24-25]
- o This is a trustworthy saying: If we die with him, we will also live with him. [2 Timothy 2:11]

Wealth

Wealth is not a sign of God's blessings. Nor is it a reflection of a person's abilities. God takes care of individual needs. The purpose of short-lived earthly wealth is to teach people responsibility so that they are prepared to handle authentic wealth in Heaven.

Figure 65: Jesus answers questions concerning paying taxes to Roman authorities.

- o He did all this so you would never say to yourself, 'I have achieved this wealth with my own strength and energy.' Remember the LORD your God. He is the one who gives you power to be successful, in order to fulfill the covenant he confirmed to your ancestors with an oath. [Deuteronomy 8:17-18]
- o "So don't worry about these things, saying, 'What will we eat? What will we drink? What will we wear?' These things dominate the thoughts of unbelievers, but your heavenly Father already knows all your needs. Seek the Kingdom of God above all else, and live righteously, and he will give you everything you need." [Matthew 6:31-33]
- o "If you are faithful in little things, you will be faithful in large ones. But if you are dishonest in little things, you won't be honest with greater responsibilities. And if you are untrustworthy about worldly wealth, who will trust you with the true riches of heaven? And if you are not faithful with other people's things, why should you be trusted with things of your own? No one can serve two masters. For you will hate one and love the other; you will be devoted to one and despise the other. You cannot serve both God and money." [Luke 16:10-13]

The Word of God exists in the form of the Life of Jesus before it is written into a book by the inspiration of God.   Bible study reflects one's relationship with God. An individual's Bible study has eternal consequences, either good or bad.

- In the beginning the Word already existed. The Word was with God, and the Word was God. He existed in the beginning with God. [John 1:1-2]
- Study this Book of Instruction continually. Meditate on it day and night so you will be sure to obey everything written in it. Only then will you prosper and succeed in all you do. [Joshua 1:8]
- Jesus said to the people who believed in him, "You are truly my disciples if you remain faithful to my teachings. And you will know the truth, and the truth will set you free." [John 8:31-32]
- And I solemnly declare to everyone who hears the words of prophecy written in this book: If anyone adds anything to what is written here, God will add to that person the plagues described in this book. And if anyone removes any of the words from this book of prophecy, God will remove that person's share in the tree of life and in the holy city that are described in this book. [Revelation 22:18-19]

Figure 66: At age 12, Jesus is teaching elders in the synagogue.

People do not live by bread alone, but by every word that comes from the mouth of God.
                                                                    --Matthew 4:4

CHRISTIAN BELIEFS

The Bible and best historical evidence present the following beliefs.

God

God is spirit. God is love. God separates the light from the dark, and God is the light.
- o "For God is Spirit, so those who worship him must worship in spirit and in truth." [John 4:24]
- o But anyone who does not love does not know God, for God is love. [1 John 4:8]
- o And God saw that the light was good. Then he separated the light from the darkness. [Genesis 1:4]
- o This is the message we heard from Jesus and now declare to you: God is light, and there is no darkness in him at all. [1 John 1:5]

Manifestations of God

God has three manifestations, called the Trinity.

(1) God's Authority is identified as "LORD" or "Father."
- o The earth is the LORD's, and everything in it. The world and all its people belong to him. [Psalm 24:1]
- o "He is the God who made the world and everything in it. Since he is Lord of heaven and earth, he doesn't live in man-made temples, and human hands can't serve his needs—for he has no needs. He himself gives life and breath to everything, and he satisfies every need." [Acts 17:24-25]

(2) God's Compassion is identified as "The Angel of the Lord" or "Jesus the Son."
- o Grace, mercy, and peace, which come from God the Father and from Jesus Christ— the Son of the Father—will continue to be with us who live in truth and love. [2 John 1:3]
- o "The Father and I are one." [John 10:30]

(3) God's Assistance to mankind is identified as "The Spirit of the Lord", "The Holy Spirit" or the "Comforter."
- o "But when the Father sends the Advocate as my representative—that is, the Holy Spirit—he will teach you everything and will remind you of everything I have told you." [John 14:26]

People

God created each person in His image so that each person can have a relationship with God.
- o So God created human beings in his own image. In the image of God he created them; male and female he created them. [Genesis 1:27]
- o Acknowledge that the LORD is God! He made us, and we are his. We are his people, the sheep of his pasture. [Psalm 100:3]
- o From one man he created all the nations throughout the whole earth. He decided beforehand when they should rise and fall, and he determined their boundaries. [Acts 17:26]

Characteristics of People

Each person has three manifestations. One might think of the Body as the clothing of the Soul, and the Soul as the clothing of the Spirit.

(1) Each person's physical being is identified as "body" or "flesh." It is not eternal.

- o Don't you realize that your body is the temple of the Holy Spirit, who lives in you and was given to you by God? You do not belong to yourself, for God bought you with a high price. So you must honor God with your body. [1 Corinthians 6:19-20]

(2) Each person's personality, decision-making processes and individuality are identified as "mind" or "soul." It is your intangible identity and survives death.

- o So letting your sinful nature control your mind leads to death. But letting the Spirit control your mind leads to life and peace. [Romans 8:6]

(3) The spiritual center of each person communicates our true and deepest loyalties and intentions, and is identified as "heart" or "spirit." Believers have a heart unified with God.

- o "Listen, O Israel! The LORD is our God, the LORD alone. And you must love the LORD your God with all your heart, all your soul, and all your strength." [Deuteronomy 6:4-5]
- o "But this is the new covenant I will make with the people of Israel on that day," says the LORD. "I will put my instructions deep within them, and I will write them on their hearts. I will be their God, and they will be my people." [Jeremiah 31:33]

Sin

People sin by rebelling against God and His authority. This offends God. With the single exception of Jesus Christ, everyone that has ever lived has sinned.

- o The LORD observed the extent of human wickedness on the earth, and he saw that everything they thought or imagined was consistently and totally evil. So the LORD was sorry he had ever made them and put them on the earth. It broke his heart. [Genesis 6:5-6]
- o For everyone has sinned; we all fall short of God's glorious standard. [Romans 3:23]
- o When Adam sinned, sin entered the world. Adam's sin brought death, so death spread to everyone, for everyone sinned. [Romans 5:12]

Sacrifice

The only way for an individual to restore the broken relationship with God is to show God he or she cares through a sacrificial gift, thus positioning oneself for proper worship.

- o When it was time for the harvest, Cain presented some of his crops as a gift to the LORD. Abel also brought a gift—the best of the firstborn lambs from his flock. The LORD accepted Abel and his gift, but he did not accept Cain and his gift. This made Cain very angry, and he looked dejected. [Genesis 4:3-5]
- o And so, dear brothers and sisters, I plead with you to give your bodies to God because of all he has done for you. Let them be a living and holy sacrifice—the kind he will find acceptable. This is truly the way to worship him. [Romans 12:1]
- o

Jesus is the One Permanent Sacrifice

People are unable to provide a sacrifice good enough, so God provides the sacrifice: His Son, Jesus.

- o But there is a great difference between Adam's sin and God's gracious gift. For the sin of this one man, Adam, brought death to many. But even greater is God's wonderful grace and his gift of forgiveness to many through this other man, Jesus Christ. And the result of God's gracious gift is very different from the result of that one man's sin. For Adam's sin led to condemnation, but God's free gift leads to our being made right with God, even though we are guilty of many sins.[Romans 5:15-16]
- o For God's will was for us to be made holy by the sacrifice of the body of Jesus Christ, once for all time. Under the old covenant, the priest stands and ministers before the altar day after day, offering the same sacrifices again and again, which can never take away sins. But our High Priest offered himself to God as a single sacrifice for sins, good for all time. Then he sat down in the place of honor at God's right hand. [Hebrews 10:10-12]

Jesus, the Son of Man, is the only Begotten Son of God

Jesus demonstrates his deity by working miracles and overcoming death.

- o Though he was God, he did not think of equality with God as something to cling to. Instead, he gave up his divine privileges; he took the humble position of a slave and was born as a human being. When he appeared in human form, he humbled himself in obedience to God and died a criminal's death on a cross. [Philippians 2:6-8]
- o This miraculous sign at Cana in Galilee was the first time Jesus revealed his glory. And his disciples believed in him. [John 2:11]
- o Jesus traveled throughout the region of Galilee, teaching in the synagogues and announcing the Good News about the Kingdom. And he healed every kind of disease and illness. [Matthew 4:23]
- o This is how Jesus the Messiah was born. His mother, Mary, was engaged to be married to Joseph. But before the marriage took place, while she was still a virgin, she became pregnant through the power of the Holy Spirit. [Matthew 1:18]

Jesus is fully God and fully Man

Jesus explains that He is both God and Man in order to claim blood relation with mankind as well as deity with God.

- o But Jesus remained silent. Then the high priest said to him, "I demand in the name of the living God--tell us if you are the Messiah, the Son of God." Jesus replied, "You have said it. And in the future you will see the Son of Man seated in the place of power at God's right hand and coming on the clouds of heaven."[Matthew 26:63-64]
- o Christ is the visible image of the invisible God. He existed before anything was created and is supreme over all creation, for through him God created everything in the heavenly realms and on earth. He made the things we can see and the things we can't see—such as thrones, kingdoms, rulers, and authorities in the unseen world. Everything was created through him and for him. [Colossians 1:15-16]

Crucifixion

The Sacrifice that God provides for us consists of the suffering and crucifixion of Jesus. This Sacrifice is sufficient to make amends for all the pain people have inflicted on God through sin (rebellion).

- o And all the people yelled back, "We will take responsibility for his death—we and our children!" So Pilate released Barabbas to them. He ordered Jesus flogged with a lead-tipped whip, then turned him over to the Roman soldiers to be crucified. [Matthew 27:25-26]
- o For God's will was for us to be made holy by the sacrifice of the body of Jesus Christ, once for all time.[Hebrews 10:10]

Resurrection

Jesus dies, is buried, and comes back to life in order to demonstrate that He is the Son of God, because only God can overcome death.

- o Pilate replied, "Take guards and secure it the best you can." So they sealed the tomb and posted guards to protect it. [Matthew 27:66]
- o Then the angel spoke to the women. "Don't be afraid!" he said. "I know you are looking for Jesus, who was crucified. He isn't here! He is risen from the dead, just as he said would happen. Come, see where his body was lying." [Matthew 28:5-6]
- o He was buried, and he was raised from the dead on the third day, just as the Scriptures said. [1 Corinthians 15:4]

Figure 67: An angel announces that Jesus is risen from the dead to two women who are followers of Jesus.

Ascension

For the purpose of His ministry on Earth, Jesus comes from Heaven to be on Earth, then ascends back to Heaven.

Figure 68: Jesus ascends to Heaven, leaving the Holy Spirit in the hearts of Believers.

- o When the Lord Jesus had finished talking with them, he was taken up into heaven and sat down in the place of honor at God's right hand. [Mark 16:19]
- o After saying this, he was taken up into a cloud while they were watching, and they could no longer see him. As they strained to see him rising into heaven, two white-robed men suddenly stood among them. "Men of Galilee," they said, "why are you standing here staring into heaven? Jesus has been taken from you into heaven, but someday he will return from heaven in the same way you saw him go! [Acts 1:9-11]

Salvation

When an individual humbly confesses their sinful nature and proclaims the sacrifice and resurrection of Jesus, the Holy Spirit of God enters them and their relationship with God is restored. In other words, they are reborn in their heart and saved from a life without God. Their reborn spirit is now one with God and they live forever.

- o If you confess with your mouth that Jesus is Lord and believe in your heart that God raised him from the dead, you will be saved. For it is by believing in your heart that you are made right with God, and it is by confessing with your mouth that you are saved. [Romans 10:9-10]
- o For you have been born again, but not to a life that will quickly end. Your new life will last forever because it comes from the eternal, living word of God. [1 Peter 1:23]
- o "I am praying not only for these disciples but also for all who will ever believe in me through their message. I pray that they will all be one, just as you and I are one—as you are in me, Father, and I am in you. And may they be in us so that the world will believe you sent me." [John 17:20-21]

Glorified Existence

From the moment of salvation, the Holy Spirit enters the Believer's heart and assists them in his or her struggle against sin, and he or she lives now and forever in Heaven.

- o For he raised us from the dead along with Christ and seated us with him in the heavenly realms because we are united with Christ Jesus. [Ephesians 2:6]
- o And we believers also groan, even though we have the Holy Spirit within us as a foretaste of future glory, for we long for our bodies to be released from sin and suffering. We, too, wait with eager hope for the day when God will give us our full rights as his adopted children, including the new bodies he has promised us. [Romans 8:23]

Fellowship within Christianity

A Christian is a disciple of Christ. Christians hold similar beliefs based on the demonstration and teaching ministry of Jesus.

- o When he found him, he brought him back to Antioch. Both of them stayed there with the church for a full year, teaching large crowds of people. (It was at Antioch that the believers were first called Christians.) [Acts 11:26]
- o Respect everyone, and love your Christian brothers and sisters. Fear God, and respect the king. [1 Peter 2:17]

Equality in Opportunity

All people are eligible to benefit from Jesus' sacrifice through belief in His resurrection.

- o "For God loved the world so much that he gave his one and only Son, so that everyone who believes in him will not perish but have eternal life." [John 3:16]
- o There is no longer Jew or Gentile, slave or free, male and female. For you are all one in Christ Jesus. [Galatians 3:28]

The Bible

The Bible is God's autobiography, written to communicate God's love to mankind. The Bible, therefore, is the final authority in all matters of faith and practice.

- o All Scripture is inspired by God and is useful to teach us what is true and to make us realize what is wrong in our lives. It corrects us when we are wrong and teaches us to do what is right. God uses it to prepare and equip his people to do every good work. [2 Timothy 3:16-17]
- o Above all, you must realize that no prophecy in Scripture ever came from the prophet's own understanding, or from human initiative. No, those prophets were moved by the Holy Spirit, and they spoke from God. [2 Peter 1:20-21]

APOLOGETICS AND EVANGELISM

Christian's are responsible for carrying God's message to others. Apologetics does not mean apologizing for Christianity. Apologetics comes from the Greek word "apologia" which means "to give a defense." The word evangelism means carrying the message of good news. This chapter provides simple answers to some of the arguments used against Christianity. Enemies, including Satan, worldly culture, and each individual's self-centered nature, attempt to persuade Believers to disavow God's authority.

- o And if someone asks about your Christian hope, always be ready to explain it. But do this in a gentle and respectful way. [1 Peter 3:15-16]
- o Therefore, go and make disciples of all the nations, baptizing them in the name of the Father and the Son and the Holy Spirit. [Matthew 28:19]

Concern #1: Hell is Unfair

Unbelievers may be convinced that a God of love wouldn't condemn people to unending punishment. Punishment is not the issue. Acceptance and rejection is the issue. If you reject Jesus, you won't be allowed to live with Him, and Jesus lives in Heaven. A contemptuous nature toward God is called blasphemy and cannot be ignored. Who in Heaven would want to coexist with people who hate God? It wouldn't be heaven!

- o "I tell you the truth, all sin and blasphemy can be forgiven, but anyone who blasphemes the Holy Spirit will never be forgiven. This is a sin with eternal consequences." [Mark 3:28-29]
- o Remember, we will all stand before the judgment seat of God. For the Scriptures say, "As surely as I live," says the LORD, every knee will bend to me, and every tongue will confess and give praise to God. [Romans 14:10-11]
- o For we must all stand before Christ to be judged. We will each receive whatever we deserve for the good or evil we have done in this earthly body. [2 Corinthians 5:10]

God wants wicked people to repent and be saved.

- o As surely as I live, says the Sovereign LORD, I take no pleasure in the death of wicked people. I only want them to turn from their wicked ways so they can live. Turn! Turn from your wickedness, O people of Israel! Why should you die? [Ezekiel 33:11]

Concern #2: What about people who never hear about Jesus?

God takes a person's knowledge into account when judging him or her. God is both just and merciful. He condemns wrongdoing, but gives everyone a chance to change and doesn't condemn people for things which are truly outside of their control.

- They know the truth about God because he has made it obvious to them. For ever since the world was created, people have seen the earth and sky. Through everything God made, they can clearly see his invisible qualities—his eternal power and divine nature. So they have no excuse for not knowing God. [Romans 1:19-20]
- They know God's justice requires that those who do these things deserve to die, yet they do them anyway. Worse yet, they encourage others to do them, too. [Romans 1:32]
- They demonstrate that God's law is written in their hearts, for their own conscience and thoughts either accuse them or tell them they are doing right. [Romans 2:15]

Concern #3: God orders the death of groups of people.

God limits sin through consequences. Cities are destroyed when the citizens are never going to repent. The righteous are spared from the destruction.

- "For we are about to destroy this city completely. The outcry against this place is so great it has reached the LORD, and he has sent us to destroy it." [Genesis 19:13]
- At dawn the next morning the angels became insistent. "Hurry," they said to Lot. "Take your wife and your two daughters who are here. Get out right now, or you will be swept away in the destruction of the city!" [Genesis 19:15]

Figure 69: Lot and his family flee as Sodom and Gomorrah burn.

Children of a sin-filled culture will grow up repeating the same wrong-doing. Children suffer the earthly consequences of their society, but do not experience the eternal consequences of adult decisions.

- The person who sins is the one who will die. The child will not be punished for the parent's sins, and the parent will not be punished for the child's sins. Righteous people will be rewarded for their own righteous behavior, and wicked people will be punished for their own wickedness. [Ezekiel 18:20]

People don't have the right to take a human life. God does have that right, however, since He has the power to bring them back to life, or place them in any sort of after-life He chooses. By proxy, a government appointed by God also has the right to take a human life.

- "You must not murder." [Exodus 20:13]
- The LORD gives both death and life; He brings some down to the grave but raises others up. [1 Samuel 2:6]
- Everyone must submit to governing authorities. For all authority comes from God, and those in positions of authority have been placed there by God. [Romans 1:1]

People are not punished for Adam's sin, called the Original sin, nor for the sins of their ancestors. Individuals are only punished for their own sin. All people, however, inherit a rebellious base nature (i.e. body of flesh) that started with Adam. We call this original sin by Adam the "Fall" of mankind. People perpetuate it through a fleshly desire to yield to temptation, but no one is forced to sin. You can choose to resist temptation and avoid sin.

- The person who sins is the one who will die. The child will not be punished for the parent's sins, and the parent will not be punished for the child's sins. Righteous people will be rewarded for their own righteous behavior, and wicked people will be punished for their own wickedness. [Ezekiel 18:20]
- You must not bow down to them or worship them, for I, the LORD your God, am a jealous God who will not tolerate your affection for any other gods. I lay the sins of the parents upon their children; the entire family is affected—even children in the third and fourth generations of those who reject me. [Exodus 20:5]
- He will judge everyone according to what they have done. [Romans 2:6]
- Temptation comes from our own desires, which entice us and drag us away. [James 1:14]
- Don't you realize that you become the slave of whatever you choose to obey? You can be a slave to sin, which leads to death, or you can choose to obey God, which leads to righteous living. [Romans 6:16]

Creation was also affected by the Fall. People have dominion over the world, which means that mankind has the authority to either bless it or curse it. As governors of the world, our sin opens access for death, disease, famine, and natural disasters to enter creation.

- Then God blessed them and said, "Be fruitful and multiply. Fill the earth and govern it. Reign over the fish in the sea, the birds in the sky, and all the animals that scurry along the ground." [Genesis 1:28]
- My experience shows that those who plant trouble and cultivate evil will harvest the same. [Job 4:8]

We are God's children at birth, born pure in spirit, but we inherit a body of flesh that has been corrupted by ancestral sin. When a person experiences temptation in the fallen world, and then chooses to sin, they offend God and must be forgiven and reborn into the perfect, faithful spirit of a child by accepting Jesus at their Redeemer. This is salvation.

- Since we respected our earthly fathers who disciplined us, shouldn't we submit even more to the discipline of the Father of our spirits, and live forever? [Hebrews 12:9]
- Jesus replied, "I tell you the truth, unless you are born again, you cannot see the Kingdom of God." [John 3:3]
- But there is a great difference between Adam's sin and God's gracious gift. For the sin of this one man, Adam, brought death to many. But even greater is God's wonderful grace and his gift of forgiveness to many through this other man, Jesus Christ. [Romans 5:15]

Concern #5: God's requirement of a sacrifice is uncivilized and inhumane.

All cultures enact consequences for misbehavior in order to (1) teach the offender; (2) protect the offended; and (3) warn potential offenders. "Sacrifice" is another way to say "consequences for bad behavior." The "bad behavior" is called sin, which mankind inherits from the Fall. The offended party is God, so the Sacrifice makes amends to God. God put forth His Son as the final sacrifice so that we could live with Him in joy. All God wants is for us to believe and obey.

- Acquitting the guilty and condemning the innocent—both are detestable to the LORD. [Proverbs 17:15]
- But Samuel replied, "What is more pleasing to the LORD: your burnt offerings and sacrifices or your obedience to his voice? Listen! Obedience is better than sacrifice, and submission is better than offering the fat of rams." [1 Samuel 15:22]
- If that had been necessary, Christ would have had to die again and again, ever since the world began. But now, once for all time, he has appeared at the end of the age to remove sin by his own death as a sacrifice. [Hebrews 9:26]

The word "sacrifice" comes from the Latin for "that which makes holy." The purpose of mankind is to learn to be holy as God is holy.

- No one is holy like the LORD! There is no one besides you; there is no Rock like our God. [1 Samuel 2:2]
- I am writing to God's church in Corinth, to you who have been called by God to be his own holy people. He made you holy by means of Christ Jesus, just as he did for all people everywhere who call on the name of our Lord Jesus Christ, their Lord and ours. [1 Corinthians 1:2]

Concern #6: God and Science are Mutually Exclusive. The world wasn't created in six days.

Some people find incongruity between the six days of God's creation at the beginning of Genesis and the discoveries of science concerning the Earth's origin. Believers disagree about the use of the Hebrew word for "day", Yom. Yom is used in the Bible to indicate a 24-hour period, a 12-hour period, today, forever, an age, a life span, or perpetuity. Multiple meanings for ancient Hebrew words are common because of the small number of words. For example, English has about 500,000 words; French has about 40,000 words; but Ancient Hebrew only has around 8,700 words. There are ongoing discoveries in archaeology, linguistics, and earth science that will continue to provide mankind with new understandings about age old questions.

- God called the light "day" and the darkness "night." And evening passed and morning came, marking the first day. [Genesis 1:5]
- For you, a thousand years are as a passing day, as brief as a few night hours. [Psalm 90:4]
- But you must not forget this one thing, dear friends: A day is like a thousand years to the Lord, and a thousand years is like a day. [2 Peter 3:8]

Some claim that Jesus is a prophet or teacher, but not part of the Godhead. Since Jesus clearly claims to be God, He's either Lord, lunatic, or liar.

- o The woman said, "I know the Messiah is coming—the one who is called Christ. When he comes, he will explain everything to us." Then Jesus told her, "I AM the Messiah!" [John 4:25]
- o You call me 'Teacher' and 'Lord,' and you are right, because that's what I am. [John 13:13]
- o But Jesus was silent and made no reply. Then the high priest asked him, "Are you the Messiah, the Son of the Blessed One?" Jesus said, "I AM. And you will see the Son of Man seated in the place of power at God's right hand and coming on the clouds of heaven." [Mark 14:60]

The prophecies, miracles, signs, and wonders confirm Jesus is Lord.

- o For a child is born to us, a son is given to us. The government will rest on his shoulders. And he will be called: Wonderful Counselor, Mighty God, Everlasting Father, Prince of Peace. [Isaiah 9:6]
- o But I have a greater witness than John—my teachings and my miracles. The Father gave me these works to accomplish, and they prove that he sent me. [John 5:36]
- o And God confirmed the message by giving signs and wonders and various miracles and gifts of the Holy Spirit whenever he chose. [Hebrews 2:4]

Jewish Leaders conspire and tell lies so they can avoid believing Jesus is God.

- o So for the second time they called in the man who had been blind and told him, "God should get the glory for this, because we know this man Jesus is a sinner." "I don't know whether he is a sinner," the man replied. "But I know this: I was blind, and now I can see!" [John 9:24-25]
- o The next day, on the Sabbath, the leading priests and Pharisees went to see Pilate. They told him, "Sir, we remember what that deceiver once said while he was still alive: 'After three days I will rise from the dead.' So we request that you seal the tomb until the third day. This will prevent his disciples from coming and stealing his body and then telling everyone he was raised from the dead! If that happens, we'll be worse off than we were at first." [Matthew 27:62-64]

Concern #8: God choosing Israel as His Chosen People is ungodly Favoritism

God chooses people based upon obedience and willingness. His chosen people are only blessed if they obey; otherwise they are cursed. God does not show favoritism and starts to attract Gentiles.

- o "Listen, O Israel! The LORD is our God, the LORD alone. [Deuteronomy 6:4]
- o For you are a holy people, who belong to the LORD your God. Of all the people on earth, the LORD your God has chosen you to be his own special treasure.
- o "Look, today I am giving you the choice between a blessing and a curse! You will be blessed if you obey the commands of the LORD your God that I am giving you today. But you will be cursed if you reject the commands of the LORD your God and turn away from him and worship gods you have not known before. [Deuteronomy 11:26-28]
- o For the LORD your God is the God of gods and Lord of lords. He is the great God, the mighty and awesome God, who shows no partiality and cannot be bribed. [Deuteronomy 10:17]
- o Then Peter replied, "I see very clearly that God shows no favoritism. In every nation he accepts those who fear him and do what is right. [Acts 10:34-35]
- o Even as Peter was saying these things, the Holy Spirit fell upon all who were listening to the message. The Jewish believers who came with Peter were amazed that the gift of the Holy Spirit had been poured out on the Gentiles too. [Acts 10:44-45]

While all of the tribes of Israel are part of the original promise of being God's chosen, only the Jews (i.e. people of Judah) have survived throughout history as a recognizable group among all of the tribes. So, history and scriptures started to also refer to the Israelite remnant as Jews. The southern tribes of Judah and Benjamin will be reunited with the dispersed tribes from Northern Israel before the End of the Age. However, it is by belief, not birth, that we are admitted into God's Kingdom. God has consistently made clear that our choice to love God is what makes us a chosen person.

- o I will gather the people of Israel from among the nations. I will bring them home to their own land from the places where they have been scattered. I will unify them into one nation on the mountains of Israel. One king will rule them all; no longer will they be divided into two nations or into two kingdoms. They will never again pollute themselves with their idols and vile images and rebellion, for I will save them from their sinful backsliding. I will cleanse them. Then they will truly be my people, and I will be their God. [Ezekiel 37: 21-23]
- o For you are not a true Jew just because you were born of Jewish parents or because you have gone through the ceremony of circumcision. No, a true Jew is one whose heart is right with God. And true circumcision is not merely obeying the letter of the law; rather, it is a change of heart produced by God's Spirit. And a person with a changed heart seeks praise from God, not from people. [Romans 2:28-29]

God has three manifestations, called the Trinity or Triune God. An analogy is illustrated in people. Simply, a person might be a father, a son, and an uncle or brother, but it is still only one person even though that one person is perceived in different roles. Spiritually speaking, each individual has (1) a body, or physical aspect; (2) a mind, or mental and emotional aspect; and (3) a soul, or spiritual aspect. The three aspects, or manifestations, of God are identified as (1) Authority; (2) Compassion; and (3) Assistance to mankind.

(1) God's Authority is identified as "LORD" or "Father."
- The earth is the LORD's, and everything in it. The world and all its people belong to him. [Psalm 24:1]
- "He is the God who made the world and everything in it. Since he is Lord of heaven and earth, he doesn't live in man-made temples, and human hands can't serve his needs—for he has no needs. He himself gives life and breath to everything, and he satisfies every need." [Acts 17:24-25]

(2) God's Compassion is identified as "The Angel of the LORD" or "Jesus the Son." Note that Jesus is not an angel and not to be confused with "An angel of the Lord."
- There the angel of the LORD appeared to him in a blazing fire from the middle of a bush. Moses stared in amazement. Though the bush was engulfed in flames, it didn't burn up. [Exodus 3:2]
- Christ is the visible image of the invisible God. He existed before anything was created and is supreme over all creation, for through him God created everything in the heavenly realms and on earth. He made the things we can see and the things we can't see—such as thrones, kingdoms, rulers, and authorities in the unseen world. Everything was created through him and for him. [Colossians 1:15-16]

(3) God's Assistance to mankind is identified as "The Spirit of the LORD" or "The Holy Spirit."
- The Spirit of the Sovereign LORD is upon me, for the LORD has anointed me to bring good news to the poor. He has sent me to comfort the brokenhearted and to proclaim that captives will be released and prisoners will be freed. [Isaiah 61:1]
- "But when the Father sends the Advocate as my representative—that is, the Holy Spirit—he will teach you everything and will remind you of everything I have told you." [John 14:26]

Concern #10: The Bible is copied from pagan myths

God puts information about Himself in every heart, so people can expect similar stories and concepts across cultures. For example, family, friends, government, worship, cause and effect, behavior and consequences are found among all people groups world-wide.

- o **Anyone who wants to do the will of God will know whether my teaching is from God or is merely my own. Those who speak for themselves want glory only for themselves, but a person who seeks to honor the one who sent him speaks truth, not lies. [John 7:17-18]**
- o **"From one man he created all the nations throughout the whole earth. He decided beforehand when they should rise and fall, and he determined their boundaries. His purpose was for the nations to seek after God and perhaps feel their way toward him and find him—though he is not far from any one of us." [Acts 17:26-27]**

All religions have some truth, or no one would believe them. That's why the enemy uses counterfeit ideas, similar to the real ones, to pull Believers away from God. For instance, the antichrist beast from the book of Revelation will provide a counterfeit resurrection that will emulate the sacrificial death and resurrection of Jesus Christ, the real Son of God.

- o **Then the angel spoke to the women. "Don't be afraid!" he said. "I know you are looking for Jesus, who was crucified. He isn't here! He is risen from the dead, just as he said would happen. Come, see where his body was lying. And now, go quickly and tell his disciples that he has risen from the dead, and he is going ahead of you to Galilee. You will see him there. Remember what I have told you." [Matthew 28:5-7]**
- o **The beast you saw was once alive but isn't now. And yet he will soon come up out of the bottomless pit and go to eternal destruction. And the people who belong to this world, whose names were not written in the Book of Life before the world was made, will be amazed at the reappearance of this beast who had died. [Revelation 17:8]**

Unlike other religions, the Bible explains the meaning of events in the context of God's Plan.

- o **"I knew you before I formed you in your mother's womb. Before you were born I set you apart and appointed you as my prophet to the nations." [Jeremiah 1:5]**
- o **For God knew his people in advance, and he chose them to become like his Son, so that his Son would be the firstborn among many brothers and sisters. And having chosen them, he called them to come to him. And having called them, he gave them right standing with himself. And having given them right standing, he gave them his glory. [Romans 8:29-30]**
- o **All praise to God, the Father of our Lord Jesus Christ, who has blessed us with every spiritual blessing in the heavenly realms because we are united with Christ. Even before he made the world, God loved us and chose us in Christ to be holy and without fault in his eyes. God decided in advance to adopt us into his own family by bringing us to himself through Jesus Christ. This is what he wanted to do, and it gave him great pleasure. [Ephesians 1:3-5]**

Concern #11: Christians get away with slavery.

During biblical times and beyond, Christians own slaves. However, slavery was only allowed to be a temporary condition. The intent in both the Old or New Testament is that: (1) slaves were to be treated fairly and not cruelly; (2) poor foreigners, widows, and orphans were to be cared for, not taken as slaves; and (3) slaves have a path to freedom.

- "At the end of every third year, bring the entire tithe of that year's harvest and store it in the nearest town. Give it to the Levites, who will receive no allotment of land among you, as well as to the foreigners living among you, the orphans, and the widows in your towns, so they can eat and be satisfied. Then the LORD your God will bless you in all your work." [Deuteronomy 14:28-29]
- "If a fellow Hebrew sells himself or herself to be your servant and serves you for six years, in the seventh year you must set that servant free." [Deuteronomy 15:12]
- Masters, be just and fair to your slaves. Remember that you also have a Master—in heaven. [Colossians 4:1]

Concern #12: Morality is relative.

Morals are determined by the information that God has planted in every heart. All civilizations adopt a similar standard of right and wrong. Heroic and unselfish actions are praiseworthy; the murder of innocents, theft, and disloyalty are abhorrent. The fact that there exists a right and wrong in every society is evidence that morality is not a matter of opinion but rather a universal concept.

- But God shows his anger from heaven against all sinful, wicked people who suppress the truth by their wickedness. They know the truth about God because he has made it obvious to them. For ever since the world was created, people have seen the earth and sky. Through everything God made, they can clearly see his invisible qualities—his eternal power and divine nature. So they have no excuse for not knowing God. [Romans 1:18-20]

Concern #13: A loving God wouldn't allow evil to exist.

God wants spiritually strong children. As the ancient Israelites conquer Canaan, God leaves pagans in the land to teach each generation of Israelites how to fight in battle. The battle is also on the spiritual plane, and for similar reasons God allows for evil to exist, for a time, to teach us how to grow from our spiritual difficulties and suffering.

- o **These are the nations that the LORD left in the land to test those Israelites who had not experienced the wars of Canaan. He did this to teach warfare to generations of Israelites who had no experience in battle. [Judges 3:1-2]**
- o **Enjoy prosperity while you can, but when hard times strike, realize that both come from God. Remember that nothing is certain in this life. [Ecclesiastes 7:14]**
- o **Yet what we suffer now is nothing compared to the glory he will reveal to us later. For all creation is waiting eagerly for that future day when God will reveal who his children really are. [Romans 8:18-19]**
- o **These trials will show that your faith is genuine. It is being tested as fire tests and purifies gold—though your faith is far more precious than mere gold. So when your faith remains strong through many trials, it will bring you much praise and glory and honor on the day when Jesus Christ is revealed to the whole world. [1 Peter 1:7]**

In the process of trials and tribulations, individuals learn courage, generosity, self-sacrifice, repentance, and forgiveness, none of which would be necessary in a perfect world. In addition, leaving evil here means that mankind gets to see God demonstrate justice and mercy, which wouldn't be necessary in a perfect world.

- o **But the Lord our God is merciful and forgiving, even though we have rebelled against him. [Daniel 9:9]**
- o **Dear brothers and sisters, when troubles come your way, consider it an opportunity for great joy. For you know that when your faith is tested, your endurance has a chance to grow. So let it grow, for when your endurance is fully developed, you will be perfect and complete, needing nothing. [James 1:2-4]**
- o **But the Holy Spirit produces this kind of fruit in our lives: love, joy, peace, patience, kindness, goodness, faithfulness, gentleness, and self-control. There is no law against these things! [Galatians 5:22-23]**
- o **But you are to be perfect, even as your Father in heaven is perfect. [Matthew 5:48]**
- o **For the LORD grants wisdom! From his mouth come knowledge and understanding. He grants a treasure of common sense to the honest. He is a shield to those who walk with integrity. He guards the paths of the just and protects those who are faithful to him. Then you will understand what is right, just, and fair, and you will find the right way to go. [Proverbs 2:6-9]**

Concern #14: Why is Christianity the only way to God?

Christianity does not teach that only Christians deserve to go to heaven. Rather, it teaches that no one deserves to go to heaven, because everyone has done wrong during their life. Individuals gain admittance to heaven by accepting Jesus Christ's death as payment for their wrongs and deciding to follow Him as Lord. The principle is that Jesus is the only way to God, not any particular church or denomination. Thus, salvation is accessible to everyone and is intended by God for everyone.

Earth

- For everyone has sinned; we all fall short of God's glorious standard. [Romans 3:23]
- Let all the world look to me for salvation! For I am God; there is no other. [Isaiah 45:22]
- For it is my Father's will that all who see his Son and believe in him should have eternal life. I will raise them up at the last day." [John 6:40]

Christianity teaches that God lasts forever and that each Believer lasts forever. Worldly belief says that a civilization is more important than an individual, because a civilization could

Figure 70: The World is fading away, but Believers live forever.

last 1000 years, while an individual lasts only 75 years. Christianity says that an individual is more important than a civilization, because an individual lasts forever, while a civilization lasts only 1000 years.

- And this world is fading away, along with everything that people crave. But anyone who does what pleases God will live forever. [1 John 2:17]
- Jesus told her, "I am the resurrection and the life. Anyone who believes in me will live, even after dying. Everyone who lives in me and believes in me will never ever die. Do you believe this, Martha?" [John 11:25-26]

Concern #15: God changes. The Old and New Testaments seem like two different Gods.

Differences between the Testaments are the result of a changing audience. The truth is consistent and revealed in a way the audience can understand. For example, a small child is told at sunset that the sun is going to bed. When the child is a teenager, more explanation is required, including planetary forces and behavior. Like the sun in this example, God remains the same, but over time, mankind's understanding changes. God has always tailored His message for the needs of the people and their circumstances.

God's Character remains the same in the Old and New Testaments. God is loving:

- The LORD passed in front of Moses, calling out, "Yahweh! The LORD! The God of compassion and mercy! I am slow to anger and filled with unfailing love and faithfulness." [Exodus 34:6]
- "For God loved the world so much that he gave his one and only Son, so that everyone who believes in him will not perish but have eternal life." [John 3:16]

God judges and punishes evildoers in the Old and New Testaments:
- o "For we are about to destroy this city completely. The outcry against this place is so great it has reached the LORD, and he has sent us to destroy it." [Genesis 19:13]
- o The Son of Man will send his angels, and they will remove from his Kingdom everything that causes sin and all who do evil. And the angels will throw them into the fiery furnace, where there will be weeping and gnashing of teeth. [Matthew 13:41-42]

Mankind's spiritual growth is dependent on us loving God:
- o And you must love the LORD your God with all your heart, all your soul, and all your strength. [Deuteronomy 6:5]
- o Jesus replied, "'You must love the LORD your God with all your heart, all your soul, and all your mind.'" [Matthew 22:37]

Mankind's spiritual growth is dependent on us loving our friends:
- o "Do not seek revenge or bear a grudge against a fellow Israelite, but love your neighbor as yourself. I am the LORD." [Leviticus 19:18]
- o A second is equally important: 'Love your neighbor as yourself.' [Matthew 22:39]

Mankind's spiritual growth is dependent on us loving our enemies:
- o "If you come upon your enemy's ox or donkey that has strayed away, take it back to its owner. If you see that the donkey of someone who hates you has collapsed under its load, do not walk by. Instead, stop and help." [Exodus 23:4-5]
- o But I say, love your enemies! Pray for those who persecute you! [Matthew 5:44]

People are commanded to protect their families:
- o "For I hate divorce!" says the LORD, the God of Israel. "To divorce your wife is to overwhelm her with cruelty," says the LORD of Heaven's Armies. "So guard your heart; do not be unfaithful to your wife." [Malachi 2:16]
- o He told them, "Whoever divorces his wife and marries someone else commits adultery against her. And if a woman divorces her husband and marries someone else, she commits adultery." [Mark 10:11-12]

SPIRITUAL DISCIPLINES

The importance of spiritual disciplines is evident throughout the Bible. Engaging in spiritual disciplines is a lifelong process that can be difficult, but is guaranteed by God to fuel our joy and provide a good witness to the world.

The sixth chapter of Ephesians provides a perfect analogy of properly getting dressed by putting on the armor of God, a terrific daily discipline that could be used as you are getting dressed in the morning. Believers won't always use the same disciplines as others, but every believer is expected to engage in regular spiritual activities.

- o My child, don't reject the LORD's discipline, and don't be upset when he corrects you. For the LORD corrects those he loves, just as a father corrects a child in whom he delights. [Proverbs 3:11-12]
- o For our earthly fathers disciplined us for a few years, doing the best they knew how. But God's discipline is always good for us, so that we might share in his holiness. [Hebrews 12:10]
- o I discipline my body like an athlete, training it to do what it should. Otherwise, I fear that after preaching to others I myself might be disqualified. [1 Corinthians 9:27]
- o Let us strip off every weight that slows us down, especially the sin that so easily trips us up. [Hebrews 12:1]

Solitude – spending time alone without distractions.
- o But Jesus often withdrew to the wilderness for prayer. [Luke 5:16]

Silence – learning to appreciate silence. Exercising wisdom before exercising our tongue.
- o Be still, and know that I am God! [Psalm 46:10]
- o Even fools are thought wise when they keep silent; with their mouths shut, they seem intelligent. [Proverbs 17:28]
- o For if we could control our tongues, we would be perfect and could also control ourselves in every other way. [James 3:2]

Fasting – depriving yourself in order to more fully experience God.
- o That is why the LORD says, "Turn to me now, while there is time. Give me your hearts. Come with fasting, weeping, and mourning. [Joel 2:12]
- o And when you fast, don't make it obvious, as the hypocrites do, for they try to look miserable and disheveled so people will admire them for their fasting. I tell you the truth, that is the only reward they will ever get. [Matthew 6:16]

Study – knowledge of God's ways prepares us for work in His Kingdom.
- o The wise are mightier than the strong, and those with knowledge grow stronger and stronger. [Proverbs 24:5]
- o I will study your commandments and reflect on your ways. [Psalm 119:15]

Worship – praising God for His wonders of creation and mercy.
- Sing to the LORD, for he has done wonderful things. Make known his praise around the world. [Isaiah 12:5]
- For God is Spirit, so those who worship him must worship in spirit and in truth. [John 4:24]

Fellowship – living in harmony with God and man.
- We proclaim to you what we ourselves have actually seen and heard so that you may have fellowship with us. And our fellowship is with the Father and with his Son, Jesus Christ. [1 John 1:3]
- They worshiped together at the Temple each day, met in homes for the Lord's Supper, and shared their meals with great joy and generosity, all the while praising God and enjoying the goodwill of all the people. And each day the Lord added to their fellowship those who were being saved. [Acts 2:46-47]

Service – working within the Kingdom of God.
- After washing their feet, he put on his robe again and sat down and asked, "Do you understand what I was doing? You call me 'Teacher' and 'Lord,' and you are right, because that's what I am. And since I, your Lord and Teacher, have washed your feet, you ought to wash each other's feet. I have given you an example to follow. Do as I have done to you. I tell you the truth, slaves are not greater than their master. Nor is the messenger more important than the one who sends the message. Now that you know these things, God will bless you for doing them. [John 12:12-17]

Prayer – sharing your heart with God.
- "When you pray, don't be like the hypocrites who love to pray publicly on street corners and in the synagogues where everyone can see them. I tell you the truth, that is all the reward they will ever get. But when you pray, go away by yourself, shut the door behind you, and pray to your Father in private. Then your Father, who sees everything, will reward you. [Matthew 6:5-6]
- Don't worry about anything; instead, pray about everything. Tell God what you need, and thank him for all he has done. [Philippians 4:6]

Giving – being generous toward the work of God.
- Yes, you will be enriched in every way so that you can always be generous. And when we take your gifts to those who need them, they will thank God. [2 Corinthians 9:11]

Meditation – listening for God and experiencing His presence.

- o Search me, O God, and know my heart; test me and know my anxious thoughts. Point out anything in me that offends you, and lead me along the path of everlasting life. [Psalm 139:23-24]
- o Study this Book of Instruction continually. Meditate on it day and night so you will be sure to obey everything written in it. Only then will you prosper and succeed in all you do. [Joshua 1:8]
- o Help me understand the meaning of your commandments, and I will meditate on your wonderful deeds. [Psalm 119:27]

Confession – being transparent and honest with other believers and God.

- o People who conceal their sins will not prosper, but if they confess and turn from them, they will receive mercy. [Proverbs 28:13]
- o "O LORD, God of Israel, you are just. We come before you in our guilt as nothing but an escaped remnant, though in such a condition none of us can stand in your presence." While Ezra prayed and made this confession, weeping and lying face down on the ground in front of the Temple of God, a very large crowd of people from Israel—men, women, and children—gathered and wept bitterly with him. [Ezra 9:15-10:1]

Resist Sin and Temptation – we must choose righteousness and ask for God's help.

- o Because he himself suffered when he was tempted, he is able to help those who are being tempted.[Hebrews 2:18]
- o The temptations in your life are no different from what others experience. And God is faithful. He will not allow the temptation to be more than you can stand. When you are tempted, he will show you a way out so that you can endure. [1 Corinthians 10:12]
- o My child, if sinners entice you, turn your back on them! [Proverbs 1:10]
- o So humble yourselves before God. Resist the Devil, and he will flee from you. [James 4:7]

All Scripture is inspired by God and is useful to teach us what is true and to make us realize what is wrong in our lives. It corrects us when we are wrong and teaches us to do what is right. [17] God uses it to prepare and equip his people to do every good work.   --2 Timothy 3:16-17

FRUITS AND GIFTS OF THE SPIRIT

     In Matthew 25 and Luke 19, Jesus teaches, through parables, on the subject of investing in the Kingdom of God. In John 6:21, He says, "Wherever your treasure is, there the desires of your heart will also be." The parables speak of how we invest our time, talent, spiritual gifts and money. Jesus is preparing our rewards according to our honest efforts as workers in the Kingdom. We are born with some talent, we apply ourselves over time, and we have some margin of worldly goods or money.

     As we mature in Christ, we produce the fruits of the Holy Spirit and exhibit Christ's character to the world as we are personally sanctified daily. The Fruits of the Holy Spirit are universal and every character of Christ is available to every believer. In Matthew 7:15-20, Jesus explains and summarizes how we can recognize people by the "fruits" they produce, concluding with, "Yes, just as you can identify a tree by its fruit, so you can identify people by their actions." Our individual character should be godly on a permanent and constant basis.

     Gifts of the Holy Spirit are specific supernatural gifts of talent or grace poured upon an individual believer to build the Kingdom and benefit others. They are not universal [1 Corinthians 12:11]. These godly supernatural gifts are dependent upon the living presence of the Holy Spirit [John 7:37-39] and are tailored for the occasion [1 Corinthians 12:6]. There are many different lists and opinions regarding spiritual gifts and we have limited our discussion to several of many.

Fruits of the Spirit
In Galatians 5:22-23 we read about the fruits from the Spirit:
  o But the Holy Spirit produces this kind of fruit in our lives: love, joy, peace, patience, kindness, goodness, faithfulness, gentleness, and self-control. There is no law against these things!

Love
  o Love is patient and kind. Love is not jealous or boastful or proud or rude. It does not demand its own way. It is not irritable, and it keeps no record of being wronged. It does not rejoice about injustice but rejoices whenever the truth wins out. Love never gives up, never loses faith, is always hopeful, and endures through every circumstance. [1 Corinthians 13:4-7]

Joy
  o You haven't done this before. Ask, using my name, and you will receive, and you will have abundant joy. [John 16:24]

Peace
  o I am leaving you with a gift--peace of mind and heart. And the peace I give is a gift the world cannot give. So don't be troubled or afraid. [John 14:27]

Patience
- Always be humble and gentle. Be patient with each other, making allowance for each other's faults because of your love. [Ephesians 4:2]

Kindness
- Don't you see how wonderfully kind, tolerant, and patient God is with you? Does this mean nothing to you? Can't you see that his kindness is intended to turn you from your sin? [Romans 2:4]

Goodness
- For this light within you produces only what is good and right and true. [Ephesians 5:9]

Faithfulness
- Let your roots grow down into him, and let your lives be built on him. Then your faith will grow strong in the truth you were taught, and you will overflow with thankfulness. [Colossians 2:7]

Gentleness
- They must not slander anyone and must avoid quarreling. Instead, they should be gentle and show true humility to everyone. [Titus 3:2]

Self-discipline
- All athletes are disciplined in their training. They do it to win a prize that will fade away, but we do it for an eternal prize. So I run with purpose in every step. I am not just shadowboxing. I discipline my body like an athlete, training it to do what it should. [1 Corinthians 9:25-27]

Gifts of the Spirit
The following are spiritual gifts gleaned from various scriptures and will give you some idea of the range and purpose of God providing spiritual gifts:

Church Planters inspire and develop churches with an apostolic spirit.
- Therefore, go and make disciples of all the nations, baptizing them in the name of the Father and the Son and the Holy Spirit. [Matthew 28:19]
- For the same God who worked through Peter as the apostle to the Jews also worked through me as the apostle to the Gentiles.[Galatians 2:8]

Prophecy is the speaking of God's truth by the power of the Holy Spirit.
- But one who prophesies is helping others grow in the Lord, encouraging and comforting them. [1 Corinthians 14:3]

Evangelism, a responsibility among all believers, is an especially effective gift for proclaiming the Gospel.

- o And you will be my witnesses, telling people about me everywhere—in Jerusalem, throughout Judea, in Samaria, and to the ends of the earth." [Acts 1:8]
- o But you should keep a clear mind in every situation. Don't be afraid of suffering for the Lord. Work at telling others the Good News, and fully carry out the ministry God has given you. [2 Timothy 4:5]

Church Leaders shepherd believers in a variety of ways.

- o Care for the flock that God has entrusted to you. Watch over it willingly, not grudgingly—not for what you will get out of it, but because you are eager to serve God. Don't lord it over the people assigned to your care, but lead them by your own good example. [1 Peter 5:2-3]

Intercessors pray in the Spirit and trusts God for the results.

- o Are any of you sick? You should call for the elders of the church to come and pray over you, anointing you with oil in the name of the Lord. Such a prayer offered in faith will heal the sick, and the Lord will make you well. And if you have committed any sins, you will be forgiven." [James 5:14-15]

Teachers communicate God's knowledge and disciple others.

- o You have heard me teach things that have been confirmed by many reliable witnesses. Now teach these truths to other trustworthy people who will be able to pass them on to others. [2 Timothy 2:2]

Discernment is knowing how to judge good from evil.

- o He gives someone else the ability to discern whether a message is from the Spirit of God or from another spirit.[1 Corinthians 12:10]

Tongues is a gift of feeling closer to God by speaking to God in an unintelligible language.

- o A person who speaks in tongues is strengthened personally, but one who speaks a word of prophecy strengthens the entire church. [1 Corinthians 14:4]

Interpretation of Tongues is the ability to publicly interpret unintelligible tongues.

- o But in a church meeting I would rather speak five understandable words to help others than ten thousand words in an unknown language.[1 Corinthians 14:19]

Hospitality is the joyful rendering of fellowship, food and lodging.

- o Cheerfully share your home with those who need a meal or a place to stay. [1 Peter 4:9]

For we know it is made acceptable by the word of God and prayer. If you explain these things to the brothers and sisters, Timothy, you will be a worthy servant of Christ Jesus, one who is nourished by the message of faith and the good teaching you have followed. Do not waste time arguing over godless ideas and old wives' tales. Instead, train yourself to be godly.   -- 1 Timothy 4:5-7

THE BODY OF CHRIST ON EARTH

Jesus dwells in heaven, interceding for us, while Believers act in His behalf on earth after asking His Spirit to dwell within the Believer.

- o **The Spirit of God, who raised Jesus from the dead, lives in you.** [Romans 8:11]
- o **Who then will condemn us? No one—for Christ Jesus died for us and was raised to life for us, and he is sitting in the place of honor at God's right hand, pleading for us.** [Romans 8:34]
- o **Don't you realize that all of you together are the temple of God and that the Spirit of God lives in you?** [1 Corinthians 3:16]

Christ is the head of the church on earth.

- o **Christ is also the head of the church, which is his body.** [Colossians 1:18]

Each of us play a role in the body of Christ.

- o **Instead, we will speak the truth in love, growing in every way more and more like Christ, who is the head of his body, the church. [16] He makes the whole body fit together perfectly. As each part does its own special work, it helps the other parts grow, so that the whole body is healthy and growing and full of love.** [Ephesians 4:14-16]
- o **All of you together are Christ's body, and each of you is a part of it.** [1 Corinthians 12:27]
- o **Just as our bodies have many parts and each part has a special function, so it is with Christ's body. We are many parts of one body, and we all belong to each other.** [Romans 12:4-5]
- o **The human body has many parts, but the many parts make up one whole body. So it is with the body of Christ. Some of us are Jews, some are Gentiles, some are slaves, and some are free. But we have all been baptized into one body by one Spirit, and we all share the same Spirit. Yes, the body has many different parts, not just one part. If the foot says, "I am not a part of the body because I am not a hand," that does not make it any less a part of the body. And if the ear says, "I am not part of the body because I am not an eye," would that make it any less a part of the body? If the whole body were an eye, how would you hear? Or if your whole body were an ear, how would you smell anything?** [1 Corinthians 12:12-17]

God commands us to be of one heart and mind in the body of Christ.

- o **There is no longer Jew or Gentile, slave or free, male and female. For you are all one in Christ Jesus.** [Galatians 3:28]
- o **"I am praying not only for these disciples but also for all who will ever believe in me through their message. I pray that they will all be one, just as you and I are one—as**

you are in me, Father, and I am in you. And may they be in us so that the world will believe you sent me. [John 17:20-21]

God works with the body of Christ to improve each soul and continue His work.
- o And remember, when you are being tempted, do not say, "God is tempting me." God is never tempted to do wrong, and he never tempts anyone else. [James 1:13]
- o Then the Lord said to Moses, "Look, I'm going to rain down food from heaven for you. Each day the people can go out and pick up as much food as they need for that day. I will test them in this to see whether or not they will follow my instructions. [Exodus 16:4]
- o Some time later, God tested Abraham's faith. "Abraham!" God called. "Yes," he replied. "Here I am." [Genesis 22:1]

Believers assemble and work cooperatively.
- o For where two or three gather together as my followers, I am there among them." [Matthew 18:20]
- o They worshiped together at the Temple each day, met in homes for the Lord's Supper, and shared their meals with great joy and generosity— all the while praising God and enjoying the goodwill of all the people. And each day the Lord added to their fellowship those who were being saved. [Acts 2:46-47]
- o If someone says, "I love God," but hates a Christian brother or sister, that person is a liar; for if we don't love people we can see, how can we love God, whom we cannot see? [1 John 4:20]
- o So encourage each other and build each other up, just as you are already doing. [1 Thessalonians 5:11]
- o Let us think of ways to motivate one another to acts of love and good works. [25] And let us not neglect our meeting together, as some people do, but encourage one another, especially now that the day of his return is drawing near. [Hebrews 10:24-25]

A FINAL WORD OF ENCOURAGEMENT

We hope our work has helped you in some way to carry on in Christ. Even seasoned veterans within the body of Christ can benefit from these clear and concise reminders of our spiritual heritage.

If you are unsure about your salvation, we urge you to find wise and honest counsel. Those people who love you the most may not feel comfortable telling you the truth. If you are a new Believer, we urge you to take these words of encouragement seriously and stay firmly on the path God has set before you.

- ❑ **Start with Prayer.**
  God freely extends Himself to assist each person with understanding, protection, and discernment as each individual acknowledges his or her relationship with Him. Spoken out-loud, each request for communication with God is answered and each individual that desires a close relationship with God is blessed.

- ❑ **Obtain a Bible and read it.**
  The text of the Bible was originally written in common local language and dialect, easily understood by the audience at the time. God implores His children to grasp His Word, so the novice Bible reader is wise to find a modern Bible translation that he or she understands well and can study frequently. Contemporary Bible translations also take advantage of recent discoveries in linguistics, archeology, and other sciences in clarifying the language of the Bible.

- ❑ **Investigate Bible Helps.**
  Just as God graciously provides doctors for the sick and advocates for the oppressed, He raises scholars and authors to assist Believers in understanding the Word. Bible helps may include dictionaries, concordances, commentaries, encyclopedias, and devotionals. None of these tools replace an individual's own Bible study, but some of them may be helpful in furthering insight and comprehension of Bible passages.

- ❑ **Associate with Believers.**
  Congregation among Believers is necessary to avoid discouragement and confusion. Each Believer finds allies using the Matthew 7:20 approach where Jesus explains, "as you can identify a tree by its fruit, so you can identify people by their actions." Although faithful church attendance may meet one's need for corporate worship, the vigilant reader seeks out additional classes and gatherings for safe and meaningful connections.

The Apostle Paul says in 2 Timothy 3:16-17 that "All Scripture is inspired by God and is useful to teach us what is true and to make us realize what is wrong in our lives. It corrects us when we are wrong and teaches us to do what is right. God uses it to prepare and equip his people to do every good work."

Bible study is the key to learning about God. The author prays that each dear reader is energized in his or her private or public ministry through Bible study.

This is a revelation from Jesus Christ, which God gave him to show his servants the events that must soon take place. He sent an angel to present this revelation to his servant John, who faithfully reported everything he saw. This is his report of the word of God and the testimony of Jesus Christ. God blesses the one who reads the words of this prophecy to the church, and he blesses all who listen to its message and obey what it says, for the time is near.   -- Revelation 1:1-3

INDEX

MEET THE AUTHOR

Chaplain Farris and Ruth Robertson, two voices that act in unison as one author, are the founders of Recovery Chapel and work with new Believers constantly. Farris disciples men in recovery from substance use disorders who have typically grown up with little or no bible knowledge. Ruth disciples women in recovery who have an array of afflictions.

Farris was saved at age 15, ventured off the holy path and squandered his blessings until age 31 when God allowed him a moment of truth in May of 1985. He has been sober since and worked through many trials and tribulations to increasingly follow Jesus. He is a writer, businessman, and minister, currently acting as the Director of a men's 43-bed long-term recovery program. His greatest satisfaction is seeing people's lives change as they begin to recognize and follow God.

Ruth grew up in a traditional modern Jewish-American family that emigrated from eastern Europe around the turn of the 20th century. Fleeing the extreme prejudice of European bigotry and violence, like many Jews, her grandparents sought the freedom and opportunity represented by American ideals. While raised with traditional Jewish values, Ruth also became aware and studied many other value systems, always interested in the spiritual aspect of existence. She had engaged with Christians, listened to them, but still didn't understand or believe that Jesus was the Messiah. In trying to read and understand the Bible, she was distraught that it was far too complex to read, that the wording was awkward, and that there seemed to be no coherent story emerging from the text.

Ruth and Farris met in 1990 and knew they had a common spiritual perspective despite their disagreement about Messiah. They married in 1991 and began to raise a family in Springfield, Missouri. Farris went to church alone early on, then with their first son. Ruth soon began attending so that she would know what their son was being taught. Over time, Ruth found the Spirit of God pulling her toward a deeper desire to uncover the truth about Messiah and the Bible. While attending a simple Bible 101, Introduction to Christianity type course, she was finally called to see that Jesus Christ is Messiah. Ruth has become an early fruit among the Jewish Believers. Farris watched with joy as Ruth and their two sons were baptized together on Palm Sunday of 2004.

Ruth still found it difficult to read certain versions of the Bible and finally settled on a translation she could appreciate. A dedicated reader and student, she found herself teaching and training new believers how to study the Bible. After years of trial and error and unwavering dedication, she developed most of the curriculum you now see here today. As a Mechanical Engineer from Georgia Tech with a MBA from the University of California at Redlands, Ruth has used her technical mind and business acumen to simplify what may seem difficult for so many... what is God trying to say to us through the Bible?

Our prayer is that you will be blessed by this effort and that your understanding will come easy.